Strategies for Winning Science Fair Projects

Joyce Henderson

Heather Tomasello

JOHN WILEY & SONS, INC.

Published by John Wiley & Sons, Inc., New York
Published simultaneously in Canada

Design and production by Navta Associates, Inc.

The publisher and the author have made every reasonable effort to insure that the experiments and activities in the book are safe when conducted as instructed but assume no responsibility for any damage caused or sustained while performing the experiments or activities in this book. Parents, guardians, and/or teachers should supervise young readers who undertake the experiments and activities in this book.

Library of Congress Cataloging-in-Publication Data

Henderson, Joyce
   Strategies for winning science fair projects / Joyce Henderson, Heather Tomasello.
      p. cm.
   Includes index.
   ISBN 0-471-41957-5 (pbk. : acid-free paper)
      1. Science projects. 2. Science—Methodology. I. Tomasello, Heather. II. Title.

   Q182.3 .H46 2002
   507'.8—dc21   2001026803

Printed in the United States of America

10 9 8 7 6 5 4 3 2 1

Strategies for Winning Science Fair Projects

Dedications

To the many talented and committed student researchers we have known, including Paul, Shawn, Jeremy, Heather, and Megan and to Ashley McGrath whose courage in the face of great challenge has inspired everyone she meets.

To J.E.H. for being a "science fair mom" and Jerel and Phil for being "writer's husbands."

Acknowledgments

Rich and Karen Regan, and Carolyn Holder, you never receive enough recognition for your inspiration and hard work with science fair students. Many thanks also to Jim Rishebarger for his years of support and encouragement, and to Dr. James Haskins and Dr. John Cech for sharing their advice and wisdom.

Contents

Introduction

Students often approach doing science fair projects with mixed emotions—excitement, enthusiasm, panic, dread. Dread because they know that these projects are intensive and time-consuming . . . in short, *hard work*. And then there is the actual fair. Standing in front of a backboard, fielding questions from judges and curious onlookers, and competing against other students can be downright nerve-racking.

So you may think we're crazy to contend that doing a science-fair project might be the most exciting, enjoyable, and educational experience that a student can undertake.

Neither of us will ever forget Heather's first successful project. She was in the sixth grade and not enthusiastic about her teacher's announcement, "Each of you must enter the school fair to pass science this year."

Like her brothers and sister, Heather had done other projects years before—growing crystals and studying eye color in her family for a genetics project—but she had never put much energy or thought into the experiments, nor won an award.

That year would be different, largely because she chose to research a question that interested her. She investigated the question, "Does a large unpopped popcorn seed produce a large popped kernel?"

Using the scientific method as her guide, she spent an entire Saturday afternoon measuring and popping kernels in an air popper, one at a time. She took careful measurements, noted the results, and wrote a paper. She enjoyed the project and she got to eat the popcorn! Her data showed that smaller unpopped kernels produced smaller popped kernels. Perhaps it was her enthusiasm, perhaps her solid use of the scientific method, or maybe the judges just liked the uniqueness of her project, but Heather won a second place at the fair. From that point on, she was hooked and participated in fairs every year until she graduated from high school.

Science research in junior and senior high school was more sophisticated than elementary-school fairs. After several years of working with various environmental projects, Heather won a special awards prize, a summer internship with a pathologist. She learned how to extract DNA and experimented with a genetic test to enhance the diagnostic staging of prostatic cancer. The project earned a first place and "Best of Show" at the district level, second place at the state level, and third place at the international fair. She also won several special awards, including a ten-day trip to Europe.

Heather's experience is not unique; countless other students participate in science research year after year. Many of these students win prizes, internships, and scholarships. They learn invaluable research skills, including how to write and deliver a scientific paper, and how to design and follow a research plan. They develop laboratory skills and master the use of statistical analysis to treat their data. Some may also learn how to use computer software programs and audio-visual equipment. They begin with simple experiments, like the popcorn project, and progress to more sophisticated research.

Basic skills apply to every project, no matter how complex. Whether you are splicing DNA or popping popcorn, you must master the scientific method, present your project to judges, learn from your mistakes, and never settle for anything but your own personal best.

As you read this book and conduct your own projects, we wish you the best of luck! Science research is not for the faint of heart. Be prepared to be challenged like never before in any other area of your life. You will find yourself spending vacations and weekends in the lab or in the classroom working on your experiment or backboard. You will be up late the night before the fair finishing graphs and logbooks. You will scramble to meet deadlines . . . deadlines . . . deadlines. And, you will learn more than you ever wanted to know about protocol.

This book is a how-to book for seventh- through twelfth-grade science research students, and their instructors and parents. School districts may define junior, middle, and senior high school levels differently. This book uses "middle" and "junior" high interchangeably and considers seventh through twelfth grade as the appropriate ages to benefit from this material.

As competitors and science fair judges, we know the strategies for successful projects. Some chapters feature insider's tips of what the judges will be looking for in every aspect of your project. We do not address the specific requirements of individual classes or competitions, such as size of the display, protocol, or methods. Our goal is to offer students direction toward choosing and developing their own projects and strategies to produce and present winning projects. Projects mentioned in this book are actual projects done by students in the past and, while you may be tempted to repeat them, do so with caution. An original project is always better.

Will following our suggestions result in winning first place at the fair every time? Probably not. We hope that you will learn that winning and success are not synonymous. Winning is a small part of the process. We hope that in studying this book, you will develop a personal definition of success and learn that not everyone can win first place. We hope that science research will impart lessons that are far more lasting and valuable than a ribbon or trophy.

Most important, though, we hope that you'll have fun in the process.

—Joyce Henderson and
Heather Tomasello

1

Why Do You Want to Be in the Science Fair?

The fact that you are reading this means that you're probably a student who is considering doing a science fair project. Maybe your teacher is requiring your entire class to do a project and your grade depends upon it. Or, perhaps you're interested in a certain field of science for your future career and want to learn more through science research. Maybe you're college-bound and have heard that science fair competitions offer scholarships, internships, and awards. You might be wondering what exactly is involved in doing a science fair project at the middle and high school level of competition. Are the results worth the time and effort?

WHAT IS INVOLVED?

In performing a science research experiment, you will be expected to select a specific topic, or research question, that you want to investigate. You'll research this area and develop an experimental plan that follows the scientific method. You'll identify the tools and materials that you need in order to actually perform the experimentation. You'll collect data, analyze the results of experimentation, form conclusions, and identify the direction that future studies may take. During the science fair you will present your work and compete against other students who have completed the same process. Along the way, you'll develop independence, initiative, and discipline.

You may be thinking, "I'll accomplish all of this just by doing a science fair project?"

You will, and probably even more! Science research is perhaps the only activity that brings together every skill and art traditionally taught separately in most junior and senior high schools. Research students must use everything that they've learned from reading, writing, math, grammar, spelling, statistics, ethics, logic, critical thinking, computer science, graphic arts, technical skills, scientific method, presentation, and public speaking. If the test of education is to teach a person to use what they have learned to move toward mastering something new, science research scores 100 percent!

Or, put more simply by Homer Hickham, former science fair winner, author and scientist, "Any time you get a large body of smart kids together and give them prizes for being smart, you've done a good thing."

THE BENEFITS

Real Life Applications. Research students are encouraged to think "outside of the box" and search for new and creative solutions to problems. You may find answers that your adult advisors have sought for years. A high school senior identified a new and more precise way to grade prostatic cancer. Her work may change treatment of several different types of cancer in the future. Another student, starting in seventh grade, spent several years examining bacterial levels in water from hundreds of backyard wells. In subsequent projects, she mapped the counts and used satellite data about the influence of weather on well contamination. City planners and water management consultants became interested in her findings. Researchers at the University of North Carolina at Charlotte are continuing the work of one student to save an endangered species of sunflower. And, the rocket-building project of a group of students in 1957 led one of them to write a book thirty years later, titled *Rocket Boys,* which was made into the movie *October Sky.*

Figure 1.1   Projects displayed at the 2000 Florida State Science and Engineering Fair. Students are selected from fairs at the regional and state levels to continue on to the "Super Bowl of Science Fairs," the Intel International Science and Engineering Fair.

Beyond the Local Competition

Certainly, much can be gained from the process of creating a science fair project and from participation in school, county, or district competitions. However, there are greater opportunities available to many students. Science research students are often encouraged to work with established scientists and educators. Fair participants are judged by local as well as world-renowned scientists, but the contact with these experts often begins long before the competition day. You may correspond with and work with scientists throughout your project. One student approached an expert in the field of biodegradation about her project and he invited her to visit his company. His lecture about the effect of quaternary ammonium compounds on carbon prompted her to ask questions and develop a project studying the bactericidal effects of quaternary ammonium salts.

Imagine the Olympics, World Series, and Super Bowl all rolled into one and you'll get an idea of the scope of the International Science and Engineering Fair. Science Service, a nonprofit organization, began sponsoring science competitions in 1950 with the International Science and Engineering Fair. Because of their vision and commitment to science research and education, millions of dollars in scholarships, grants, equipment, and trips are given to students every year. The competition, now cosponsored by Intel Corporation, involves three to five million students participating at local levels and over one thousand projects from forty-eight states and forty other nations proceed to the International Fair. Twelve hundred scientists, engineers, and professionals from every type of industry, all of whom have Ph.D.'s and at least eight years of experience, volunteer their time to serve as judges. In addition to scholarships, grants, trips, and awards that are presented to students with winning projects, the top two students are invited to attend the Nobel Prize ceremony in Stockholm, Sweden.

Science Service and the Intel Corporation also sponsor the annual Intel Science Talent Search (formerly known as Westinghouse Talent Search), the oldest and most prestigious science contest. Since 1942, this competition has provided millions of dollars in scholarships and awards. In the first 59 years of the competition, 2,240 first place finalists received more than $3.8 million in college scholarships. *Every student who participates in the Science Talent Search wins some monetary award.*

Recently, another science competition has been developed by Science Service and Discovery Communications for students in grades five through eight. The Discovery Young Scientist Challenge is open by invitation. Judges at your ISEF-affiliated fair will select nominees for the Discovery Young Scientist Challenge and prizes will be given out at your local fair, then an entry form is mailed to participants.

Scholarships, Awards, and Prizes. Students often receive scholarships and prizes because of their projects. An invitation to work with a hospital pathologist enabled two high school juniors to develop a team project examining the DNA of breast cancer that took first place at the Intel International Science and Engineering Fair. One of their awards was a trip to Greece to present their paper at an international science symposium. Another high school senior spent ten days touring Europe, all expenses paid, because of her successful science fair project on grading cancer by the shape and structure of its DNA.

College and Career Success. Science research competition is often the ticket to success in college and in a career in science. College admissions offices face the dilemma of evaluating thousands of applications from intelligent, motivated students. Colleges look for science research participation. They know that these students have the maturity, self-confidence, and the ability to solve problems that predict success in college.

In a recent survey, students listed how they think science research will help them in their academic career beyond high school:

"You learn a lot about responsibility."

"I know how to do research papers."

"It teaches you how to use a computer."

"Helps you decide what field to enter."

"Builds self-confidence and character."

"Gives interaction with others in education."

"It is an outlet to practice public speaking."

"Gives good interviewing skills."

"Increases social skills."

"Helps you know that you had a chance in your life to be somebody."

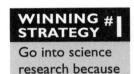

WINNING STRATEGY #1

Go into science research because you want to.

Students surveyed also revealed some of their favorite aspects of the work. One student said that he most enjoyed "doing the testing and research; experimenting." Another preferred the "competition and rewards." "The feeling of accomplishment when the project is done" was one student's response. Some enjoyed "working together with other research students." Almost all responded that "being able to gain a large amount of knowledge about something I enjoyed doing" was a favorite part of science research.

Participating in science research competition can influence the direction your life takes. The Intel Science Talent Search reports that 95 percent of former finalists have a career in some field of science. More than half became research scientists or professors at universities. Alumni also include five Nobel Prize winners, two Fields Medal awards (the equivalent of the Nobel Prize in math), three National Medal of Science winners, and scientists who have won awards from the MacArthur Foundation, Sloan Research Fellows, the National Academy of Science, and the National Academy of Engineering.

WINNING STRATEGY #2

Expect the experience to be an adventure; you will learn something new!

Who knew when she was in third grade doing a project involving tree rings that Shawn Nobles would someday receive her master's degree in Environmental Education?

Jeremy Reis was always interested in computers; his projects involving artificial intelligence led to a career in computers and web design.

THE COSTS

We would not want to miss the downside of science research. As in everything worth taking on, there are challenges and stresses. In fact, those same students surveyed had a lot to say about the difficulties encountered in completing their projects:

> "Paperwork and getting approval."
>
> "The time it consumes."
>
> "Trying to get materials."
>
> "Having to figure out what graphs to do."
>
> "Getting the project done at the last minute."
>
> "Set up for fairs—it's always the most stressful time."
>
> "Background research."
>
> "The limited time to complete project."
>
> "Waiting for judges."
>
> "Finding out that in middle school the teacher doesn't do everything for you!"

WINNING STRATEGY #3

If you never try, you never win.

In spite of all the challenges, the experiments that don't always work, the lab mice that escape confinement, the daphnia that die over Christmas break, the computer program that crashes, students do keep coming back. They may not completely understand the future benefits, but they do know why they enjoy science research. One student summed it up with this comment, "You name it, I've gained it from science research!"

WINNING STRATEGIES

1. Go into science research because you want to.
2. Expect the experience to be an adventure; you will learn something new!
3. If you never try, you never win.

2

Getting Started

Selecting a Research Topic

An Old Chinese proverb says: "A journey of a thousand miles begins with a single step." That first step in your science fair journey is choosing the topic you want to explore. This may be easier said than done. One student described this aspect of research as "the most horrible part." It's important to choose wisely. So, how do you start when you have no idea what to do?

What you need is a strategy, and there are better methods than flipping through your science textbook in a haphazard search for an idea.

AS YOU CONSIDER DIFFERENT PROJECTS, THINK ABOUT THESE QUESTIONS:

- What would be your goal in doing this project?
- What idea could you test?
- What scientific question could you answer?

NARROWING THE FIELD

You have certain unique interests and abilities. I know, you never believed your mother when she told you this, but it is true! You can narrow your search considerably by listing the things that truly interest you. (For some, it may be easier to identify what you do *not* find interesting.) Are you passionate about the environment, music, people, or chemistry? Don't worry if you feel you don't know very much about any of these things. Part of the scientific method (described in Chapter 3) involves gathering background information. By the time you're finished with your experimentation, you'll be an expert!

WINNING # 1 STRATEGY

Do a project that you will enjoy.

Figure 2.1
Do a project that interests you.

Brainstorm using the following questions. Write your answers down and refer back to them during your search:

- What are my interests? What do I find uninteresting?

- Is there anything that I've always wondered about or questioned?

- Do I prefer the "hard" sciences (physics, chemistry, mathematics) or the "soft" sciences (biology, botany, medicine, and health)?

- Is there a category of science fair competition that appeals to me more than any other? (See the end of this chapter for the International Science and Engineering Fair categories.)

- Do I prefer to spend time inside or outside?

- Is there a particular interest about which I feel passionate?

- What resources are available to me in terms of labs, research facilities, equipment, and mentors?

RESEARCHING POSSIBLE TOPICS

Now that you have some answers from your brainstorming you can return to that old science textbook, right? Well, yes and no. Some students may find inspiration for their topic in a textbook, but there are many more places to look. Scientific journals such as *Science News* and *Scientific American,* and popular magazines such as *Discover* and *Popular Science* are excellent sources for ideas. Scientific journals feature the most up-to-date research taking place in the United States and beyond. Do not be intimidated by these publications; many are very easy to read and understand.

WINNING STRATEGY #2

As you look for a topic, record exactly where you find any information. This will help you in the future when you begin to write your research paper.

Another approach is to look for a *problem* and gear your project toward solving that problem. The problem becomes the question and the solution is your hypothesis. Your interest may be triggered by a real-life situation, such as a disease that affects someone you know, an ecological concern in your own community, or your interest in a pet's behavior.

WINNING #3 STRATEGY

Consider the world around you, the problems of your family, friends, and community.

The local newspaper is an often overlooked source of valuable information. This is especially true in the area of environmental sciences. Does your community have any unique ecological challenges? For example, students in a Florida coastal county have performed experiments on drinking water pollution, beach erosion, sea turtle migration, and alien tree species. What are your hometown's sources of commerce and industry? Students have experimented with citrus crops, endangered North Carolina sunflowers, and the structure of satellites. Following the daily news of your community will you give you a sense of the specific questions that you might tackle in your project.

Finally, your own observation of the natural world is a valuable source of possible topics to investigate. You may have learned that green plants contain chlorophyll and photosynthesize. Do plants that aren't green still carry on photosynthesis? Do they contain some other pigment? Does a firefly's flash rate change depending on the outside air temperature? Do certain kinds of spiders create certain kinds of patterns in their webs? Are certain web designs more effective at catching insects than others? The world around you is full of fascinating questions that can be explored in your science fair project.

Figure 2.2
Look around your community for a possible topic.

Figure 2.3
Observing the world around you may also suggest a topic.

KEEP IT SIMPLE

Don't be afraid to select what appears to be a simple project (so long as it isn't too simple, and your teacher is the best judge of that). Not everyone can split DNA, clone a baby chick, discover a cure for a disease, test water in several thousand backyard wells, or build a robot that will revolutionize the auto industry. Sometimes it is the less sophisticated project that when well researched and presented is a winner.

One student visited the La Brea tar pits in California where she learned about the plight of birds that become trapped in the oily slick of the pits. These birds have to be cleaned one by one or they die. She wondered about a method for cleaning birds caught in an oil spill. Further research told her that thousands of birds die every time there is an oil spill. Attempts to clean them were often futile because of sheer numbers and the remoteness of many places where oil spills occur. Over the course of several years' projects, she tested different detergents and different methods of cleaning and then created a pressure washing system that was quick, easy, and efficient, and didn't harm the feather spicules which would have killed the birds. She discovered a significant, real-world problem that no one in the commercial or scientific communities had investigated. Then she experimented and developed a solution that could save birds' lives.

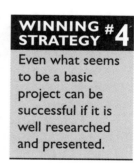

WINNING # 4 STRATEGY

Even what seems to be a basic project can be successful if it is well researched and presented.

KEEP IT NARROW

Don't allow yourself to be sidetracked with a problem that has too many aspects to pursue. You can always decide to make your project a continuing study for future years. The more narrow your focus, the more you can

**WINNING #5
STRATEGY**

It is the process
(following the
scientific method)
that makes the
project.

concentrate on the process rather than the outcome. Occasionally, your research of background information will suggest an entirely different direction in which to proceed, and you will have to decide which experiment you want to perform and whether to save the rest for another year. Choose one aspect of the problem and work to find and test one solution, even if it doesn't work.

CAUSE AND EFFECT

David Morano, an associate professor at Minnesota State University, Mankato, writes that it is the "existence of 'cause and effect' relationships in nature that makes experimental science possible."

Cause-and-effect projects state, "If you do this, then that will happen." For example, if you water these plants, they will grow; if you wear a black shirt in the sunlight, you will be warmer than if you wear a white shirt. These titles from international science fair winners show a cause-and-effect relationship demonstrated in the projects:

**WINNING #6
STRATEGY**

Select a question that
can be investigated with
experimentation that
looks at cause-and-
effect relationships.

"The Effect of Gatorade on the Metabolism
    of Male Athletes"

"The Effects of Heavy Metals on Various Plants"

"A Soil Analysis of Impacted Pond Apple Slough"

"Photodegradation of Plastic Bags"

"A Chocolate Bar a Day Keeps the Dentist Away"

PITFALLS TO AVOID

Your topic for experimentation needs to be doable. As Richard Adams and Robert Gardner write in *Ideas for Science Projects,* "It would be ridiculous to ask, 'Why is there gravity?' Or, 'Why is there air?' These questions cannot be experimentally investigated." Ask a question that can be answered through experimentation.

Pick a topic your parents and teacher will approve. Consider the materials, equipment, or supplies you will need. A list may help the teacher decide if the project can

**WINNING #7
STRATEGY**

Choose a project
that is doable.

be approved. It is not uncommon for projects today to require such sophisticated technology as a laser, electron microscope, incubator, autoclave, hyperbaric chamber, or a wind tunnel. If your school does not have what you need, is there a research lab, a university lab, or a hospital lab where you can work? Is there a mentor or research scientist willing to supervise your work? Your teacher may be able to put you in contact with the right person.

If your project requires a controlled environment over a period of time, what will happen over the Christmas holiday or school breaks? What will happen if there is loss of electricity because of a storm? Is there sufficient security for your project? One student storing chemicals in a school refrigerator was dismayed when they were thrown away, nearly ruining her project.

Speaking of chemicals, will your project involve chemicals that may be hazardous to use? Do you have personal protective attire available for your use? How will you dispose of these chemicals? Even something you may consider ordinary such as motor oil cannot be poured down the drain when you are done using it. Chemicals must be handled according to state and federal environmental rules and regulations, as well as school and ISEF guidelines. Your school should have a book listing all chemicals that may or may not be used and how to handle and dispose of them properly.

Projects involving viruses require a professional research laboratory and supervising scientist. Recombinant DNA projects must comply with National Institutes of Health guidelines. A lab and scientist must be licensed to use radioactive materials, and special shielding must be available whenever you work with a laser, ultraviolet (UV) light, X ray, microwave radiation, or high-intensity radio frequency (RF) waves. Most state science academies prohibit the use of cultures taken directly from humans or other warm-blood animals because of the danger of unknown viruses. Cultures must be purchased from reputable supply houses.

Now that you have narrowed down your topic to one or a few choices, ask a friend, classmate, or parent to review it. Ask them to apply the questions below (often another person may catch something that you never considered.)

> **WINNING STRATEGY #8**
>
> The work must be yours, but don't do it alone. Parents, teachers, and mentors can all help you succeed.

OTHER QUESTIONS TO CONSIDER AS YOU DELIBERATE OVER TOPIC IDEAS:

- Is this topic truly interesting to me? Enough so that I won't lose interest after one month or longer?

- Can my project be completed in an allotted period of time? What will be the time commitment for experimentation (two hours every afternoon, once a week, etc.)?

- Is my project safe? Do I have access to the necessary equipment and technology to perform the experiment with proper technique? Is there someone available to act as mentor?

- Is it an actual experiment and not just research in a particular area? Can I discover, study, design, create, or improve something?

- Is my project relevant? (Students often call this question, "Who cares?") Will it benefit society or my community?

- Is my project creative or original?

Jot down the pertinent information: a possible title, the question, what supplies you will need, who might be your supervising scientist or mentor. Now, it's time to present your project to your teacher. He or she will help you complete the forms necessary for approval, get together the equipment and supplies, and contact a mentor.

Table 2.1

Categories Used by the International Science and Engineering Fair

(Your school or region may use different categories. Ask your teacher for a list of categories used in your science fair.)

Behavioral and Social Sciences	Gerontology
Biochemistry	Mathematics
Botany	Medicine and Health
Chemistry	Microbiology
Computer Science	Physics
Earth and Space Sciences	Team projects
Engineering	Zoology
Environmental Science	

WINNING STRATEGIES

1. Do a project that you will enjoy.
2. As you look for a topic, record exactly where you find any information. This will help you in the future when you begin to write your research paper.
3. Consider the world around you, the problems of your family, friends, and community.
4. Even what seems to be a basic project can be successful if it is well researched and presented.
5. It is the process (following the scientific method) that makes the project.
6. Select a question that can be investigated with experimentation that looks at cause-and-effect relationships.
7. Choose a project that is doable.
8. The work must be yours, but don't do it alone. Parents, teachers, and mentors can all help you succeed.

3

There's a Method to the Madness

Using the Scientific Method

Now that you have settled on your topic, the next step is to develop your plan. To do this you will need to use the scientific method. Your experimental question is the "what" of your research, and the scientific method is the "how." Don't be intimidated by this pair of words—the scientific method is nothing more than a step-by-step logical plan used by scientists.

BASIC ELEMENTS OF A SCIENCE FAIR PROJECT

Most projects consist of the following parts:

- *Problem (may be the title of your project):* The clear, brief statement or the question(s) you want to answer through your experiment. The problem may take the form of a statement such as "The Effects of *a* on *b*." Or, the problem may be a question, "What Will Be the Effects of *a* on *b*?"

- *Hypothesis* (also known, by some students, as the "hypotheguess"): The question reworded as a statement that will be proved or disproved by the experiment. You are predicting what the results will be.

- *Purpose:* A statement of what you hope to discover through your experimentation. Within the purpose is the more specific practical application. This may be listed separately and answers the question, "Who cares?" What are some of the valuable implications of your research?

- *Background:* Information that you gather about the subject you are researching.

- *Materials:* A list of the items that you will need to carry out your research.

- *Procedure:* A step-by-step plan or recipe describing how to perform the experiment.

- *Data:* The results of your experimentation. (Statistical analysis may be required, and this is covered in greater detail in Chapter 7.)

- *Results:* A summary of the data.

- *Conclusion:* An assessment of the experiment and whether the hypothesis was supported or disproved by the results. Plans for future studies may also be described here.

NOTHING MORE THAN CHILD'S PLAY

Don't worry about using the scientific method. It's a plan for problem solving that you've been doing all your life, but didn't realize it. For example, imagine that you are three years old and there's a bag of marshmallows that you want on top of the refrigerator. You know that standing on tiptoe and stretching will not work. You look around the kitchen and spy a chair. Pushing and pulling, you move the chair to the refrigerator and climb up on it. You are still not tall enough, but you can climb from there to the counter. If you slide the toaster out from under the edge of the cabinet and balance precariously on it, you can reach the marshmallows. Here's how this experience would translate to the scientific method:

- *Problem:* Can a three-year-old reach the bag of marshmallows on top of the refrigerator?

- *Hypothesis:* A three-year-old can reach the bag of marshmallows on top of the refrigerator.

- *Purpose:* To discover whether or not a young child can build a structure in order to reach a bag of marshmallows placed on a 6-foot-high object.

- *Background:* Marshmallows are a well-loved treat for children, providing a strong incentive. The refrigerator is much taller than the child subject. However, access may be gained by using materials in the room.

- *Materials:* Refrigerator, bag of marshmallows, chair, counter, toaster

- *Procedure:*
  1. Move chair to refrigerator.
  2. Climb onto chair.
  3. Climb from chair to counter.
  4. Pull toaster out.
  5. Step up onto toaster.
  6. Reach for the bag.
  7. Rip open the bag and enjoy the marshmallows.

- *Data:* Chair alone does not provide sufficient height to reach top of refrigerator. Chair + counter + toaster = bag in hand.

- *Conclusion:* The three-year-old can reach the bag, therefore, hypothesis accepted.

PROBLEM AND HYPOTHESIS

In the scientific method, the problem and the hypothesis are directly related. Your title (or problem) asks a question while your hypothesis seeks to answer it. If your title is "What Will Be the Effects of *a* on *b*?" then your hypothesis begins simply with "*A* will affect *b* in this manner. . . ." It is the statement of what you expect to find in the experimentation or what you want to be true. Sometimes a researcher will choose to use a **null hypothesis,** which states the *opposite* outcome of what is expected. The expectation is that it will be easier to disprove an assumption than it is to prove it.

An example of a hypothesis is: "A Gerbil Can Learn to Run a Maze." The null hypothesis for the same project would be: "A Gerbil Cannot Learn to Run a Maze." In either case, the hypothesis predicts the outcome or the result of a problem.

A problem is usually phrased as a question, while the hypothesis is a statement. Examples of problems and their corresponding hypotheses are:

- *Problem:* What is the effect of nitrogen fertilizer on tomato plants? *Hypothesis:* Addition of nitrogen fertilizer to tomato plants will produce taller and more productive plants.

- *Problem:* Is soil needed to grow Spanish onions? *Hypothesis:* Spanish onions will grow faster and larger in soil than in water.

- *Problem:* Can chicken bones provide a source of dietary calcium for humans? *Hypothesis:* Chicken bones can provide dietary calcium for humans.

Remember the cause-and-effect relationship? It is easy to develop a hypothesis for a cause-and-effect project by using an "If . . . then . . ." statement.

SAMPLE HYPOTHESES AS "IF . . . THEN . . ." STATEMENTS

- *If* a tomato plant is fed fertilizer, *then* it will grow bigger and stronger than one that is not given fertilizer.

- *If* a gerbil is offered certain rewards, *then* it will learn to run a maze.

- *If* soil is used to grow Spanish onions, *then* they will grow better than those grown in water.

- *If* there is calcium in chicken bones, *then* they might be a dietary source for calcium.

WINNING # 1 STRATEGY

Keep the problem and hypothesis narrow in scope.

Often, when you begin experimenting, your natural curiosity kicks in and you want to answer a dozen more questions. Stick to just one for your project.

PURPOSE

Students often consider the purpose statement of little importance, but it can mean the difference between a good project and a winning project. The purpose explains why you are pursuing your research topic. It often includes a statement of practical application that explains the real-world value of your study. A high school senior evaluated the way a local pathology department graded prostate cancer in patients over a five-year period. She regraded slides of the cancerous tissue using a more accurate genetic test and found that human error was a factor in patient care in over 75 percent of the cases. Her research had very practical applications for the doctors in the pathology department and their patients. Additionally, she was able to educate members of her community about the genetic test as an option for diagnosis of their cancers.

WINNING #2 STRATEGY

The practical application or significance of the project can make a project superior to the rest.

BACKGROUND

After you have settled on the topic for your project, have a problem or question, and have developed the hypothesis, it's time to get down to some serious research. Researching the background information will help you begin to see the direction that your project will take. The study of facts about the subject requires use of all the resources available to you: a library, your teacher, a mentor/scientist, the Internet, newspapers, magazines, books, interviews, a visit to a research facility, encyclopedias, databases, and government publications. (In the next chapter on writing your paper, you will find information on how to handle all of the information, including how to present and credit it.)

INSIDER'S TIP

As you begin to research, it is just as important to note where you found the information as what the information is. Get in the habit now of writing down the name of the source, author's name, publisher's name, year of publication, and page number of the information.

Make a list of questions you want to answer in your research. Here are some examples of background questions about our sample projects:

- *What is the Effect of Nitrogen Fertilizer on Tomato Plants?:* Do different varieties of tomatoes grow at different rates? Are there different nitrogen fertilizers? How much nitrogen is in fertilizer? Can I isolate the nitrogen and only apply it? What other conditions affect the growth of a tomato plant? How often should I add the fertilizer? How will I fertilize the plants?

WINNING #3 STRATEGY

You will not use all the background information you learn about your subject, but the more you know, the better your project will be.

- *Can Gerbils Learn to Run a Maze?:* What is a gerbil? How are they raised? What is their life span? At what age might they learn best? What type of maze would work best? Will color or materials used make any difference? What reward or stimulus could be used to motivate the gerbil to run the maze? How will I time the gerbil's run? How many gerbils will I study?

- *Is Soil Needed to Grow Spanish onions?:* What is the plant species? What type of soil will I use? Will I start the plants from seed or buy ones that have already been started? Which fertilizer(s) should I use? How much light do the plants require? What temperature is optimal for their growth? How frequently should I water them? Over what period of time will I grow them?

- *Can Chicken Bones Provide a Source of Dietary Calcium?:* Which bone(s) will I test? How much calcium do they contain? Does the chicken's diet change the amount of calcium in its bones? What is the suggested amount of calcium needed by humans at different ages? How would a human ingest chicken bones and how much calcium would a human derive from chicken bones?

These are but a few points of those projects that can be investigated for background information. While most students are anxious to get to the "do it" stage of experimentation, the information-gathering process is far more important. It is then that you learn about your subject and what you will need to consider or include during experimentation.

MATERIALS AND PROCEDURE

Once you have researched the subject thoroughly, you should be able to develop the procedure you will follow in the experimentation. The procedure is a step-by-step recipe that anyone could follow to do your experiment. It is helpful to write it out before you begin so that you can identify the equipment and supplies you will need. This will be the **materials list.** You will want to keep your log handy to jot down the actual steps you take as you work because often you cannot identify every step in advance. The procedure needs to be very detailed, with each step in order. Think of it as giving a friend directions to your house. You would not leave out any roads or turns or identifying landmarks if you wanted that person to find your place.

You may find an idea in a book or even select an experiment from a book, but the work of doing the experiment must be entirely your own. If a new skill or procedure is required, someone may show you how to do it, but, you must then do the procedure on your own. If you need assistance, someone may assist, but you must accomplish the bulk of the work yourself.

As you plan your procedure, keep in mind that your experimentation *must* contain controls and variables. **Variables** are any factors that may affect your outcome and which can be changed. **Controls** are any factors that cannot be changed. They provide the measurement against which to compare your results. In other words, if you are doing a project involving adding fertilizer to plants, you will grow some plants with the fertilizer (the variable set) and some without (the control set.) You will then measure your experimental plants and compare them to the control plants. If fertilizer is the single variable you are examining, you will keep all other variables (such as light, water, and temperature) the same. During your research, you will want to consider all of the possible variables that may influence your project.

Examples of Variables and Controls

Variables	Controls
Type of tomato plant, soil, food, growing conditions, light, water, air movement, and time period of study	Group of plants grown in the same soil under the same growing conditions as the experimental plants but without plant food
Gerbil's age, sex, type of reward or stimulus, hunger, fatigue, the type of maze, color, temperature, other environmental factors	Gerbil who does not learn to run maze
Spanish onion plants, soil, type of plant food, growing conditions, water, light, air movement, frequency, and amount of feeding	Spanish onion plants grown in water with the same growing conditions and feeding
Bone of chicken used, sex of chicken, feed, method of extracting and measuring calcium	Chicken raised on standard chicken feed

You will want to conduct your experiment several times, or use more than one subject. Each time you do the same experiment (called a "run"), you collect information. There is no way to tell you how many runs you will need to do. Your teacher may be able to help you decide. You want to conduct the experiment as many times as is necessary to obtain sufficient data. But, at some point, you do need to stop experimenting and conclude the project.

WINNING # 4 STRATEGY
Begin your project early enough to give yourself time to do all the experimental runs. A good project can be defeated by not having enough runs and data.

DATA AND RESULTS

You have your procedure sketched out, your equipment and supplies assembled, and you are ready to conduct your experiment. Are you also prepared to measure the results? The results of the experiment are observations of either subjective or objective data. Subjective observations are whatever you observe through your senses: Gerbil A runs the fastest, Gerbil B is easily distracted along the course of the maze, Gerbil C isn't interested in the rewards at the end of the maze.

Objective observations are quantified or measured in size, weight, frequency, duration, or time. They are expressed numerically, using the metric system whenever possible. The experimental plant grew 7 centimeters taller than the control plant. Chicken thigh bones contain 8 milligrams more of calcium than breast bones. Be as exact in your measurements and observations as you can.

Whether your observations are subjective or objective, they must be recorded and the best place is in your daily log. Scraps of paper get lost, computers crash, memories don't count. In addition to recording your observations in your log, you may want to take photographs and keep them with your log as well.

Once measured and recorded, your observations become data. (How to handle data is covered in Chapter 7.) From your data, you can draw conclusions. Was your hypothesis correct? Did you prove it or disprove it?

When a hypothesis is proven to be correct it is supported. It's okay to disprove, or reject, a hypothesis. Explain thoroughly in your conclusions why the hypothesis was not proved. Your experimentation can be a complete failure, but your project can be successful if you followed scientific procedure and learned from the experiment.

INSIDER'S TIP

If you are not familiar with the metric system, this is a great time to learn it. It is the standard for scientific research. Metrics are really very simple and your teacher can help you obtain a metric ruler or scale. Be sure you don't mix up inches with centimeters, or ounces with grams. Use metrics and be consistent!

ONE STUDENT'S STORY

An eighth-grade student wanted to clean oil-contaminated duck feathers by using different detergents and different methods of cleaning. Her hypothesis was that she could clean the feathers without breaking the spicules of the feather. In her first year of study, every feather spicule was damaged and none were oil-free after cleaning. She placed first in the district and third in the state. In her next year of study, she developed a special pressure washing system for the feathers. Again, most of the feather spicules were damaged and few were oil-free. She placed first in district again and second in the state. The third year, she used bacteria that eats oil with slightly greater success. Fewer feathers were damaged and some were actually cleaned. She placed second in the district. She never succeeded in cleaning all of the oil from the feathers without damaging them, but her projects were very successful because they had practical significance, she followed the scientific method, and presented her projects well to the judges.

THE CONCLUSION

WINNING #5 STRATEGY

Rejecting a hypothesis can be just as valuable as supporting it.

In the conclusion of your project, compare and contrast the experimental group and the control group. For example, in the gerbil project, the control gerbil never learned to run the maze, but the experimental gerbil did. The gerbils were timed for several different runs on different days. When the data were studied, the researcher could draw the conclusion that a gerbil could learn to run a maze.

Experimentation doesn't end your work. You must correlate, chart, and interpret the findings in a way that others can understand. Using our gerbil project example: Gerbil A was timed, running the maze on different days, always at the same time of day. Two different rewards were offered: peanut butter and sunflower seeds. Gerbil B, the control gerbil, was put in the maze but never offered a reward. Gerbil A's time was recorded for each day and each reward. Three columns of data were recorded in the logbook: times of runs with the peanut butter reward, times with the sunflower seed reward, and the times of the control gerbil. With that information, the student determined that on successive days, the gerbil ran faster and therefore learned to run a maze. In the second part of the experiment, the student could also study which reward gave greater motivation to the gerbil to complete the maze. Simply teaching the gerbil to run a maze is an adequate, although simple, project. Adding different rewards to motivate the gerbil adds an additional dimension to the project and the opportunity for a second hypothesis and a second set of data and conclusions.

INSIDER'S TIP

You can add to the complexity of the project by studying more than one variable, however, do not allow yourself to become distracted by too many variables. Comparing two or three is sufficient to produce data and conclusions. Be sure your hypothesis reflects every variable you study. For example, if your hypothesis states a plant grown with nitrogen fertilizer will be taller and produce more flowers than a plant grown without fertilizer, you will have two sets of data, one pertaining to height of the plants, the other to the number of flowers.

Science projects begin with an idea, a question, an inspiration, an observation, and they always end with an answer that must be shared with others. Your conclusion is as valuable as the experimentation. What did you learn? How might you improve? What further study is indicated? If you repeated the project, what might you do differently?

WINNING STRATEGIES

1. Keep the problem and the hypothesis narrow in scope.

2. The practical application or significance of the project can make your project superior to the rest.

3. You will not use all the background information you learn about your subject, but the more you know, the better your project will be.

4. Begin your project early enough to give yourself time to do all the experimental runs. A good project can be defeated by not having enough runs and data.

5. Rejecting a hypothesis can be just as valuable as supporting it.

4

Who? What? Where? When? and How?

The Science Research Paper

You've chosen a topic and you have a handle on the scientific method, so you're ready to jump into the research and experimentation. Right?

No. First you need a strategy for writing your research paper. The purpose of this paper is to share your use of the scientific method with others. When all is said and done, you'll have pages full of background information, experimental procedures, data, statistical analysis, and your conclusions. Communicating this information clearly requires organization. And, you'll need to be thinking about how to do that from the very start.

Actually, you've already started working on the research paper; you just didn't realize it. The paper starts with the selection of your topic. You'll begin your research paper with your experimental question and corresponding hypothesis. You'll then go on to explain what you learned, what you did, and why. Conclude with the reasons why this subject was interesting and significant and how you might study it further in the future.

That is your research paper in a nutshell! Your statements will be supported by your background research. Your opinion and your experimentation are important, but in a scientific paper they are only worthwhile when supported by facts. To make sure you cover all the bases, think about the journalists' five questions: who, what, where, when, and why.

> **WINNING STRATEGY # 1**
>
> The research paper is not simply a listing of sources. A good paper is focused and organized. Start thinking about how you'll organize your paper before you even begin the research.

WHO?

Who is your audience? You don't write a paper for your own reading or just to have something to display with your project. Your paper reflects all the work you have done. It includes the relevant background research, the procedure you used, the results you obtained, and the lessons you have learned. To write clearly, you need to understand who your audience is and the level of presentation they want to read.

When writing a research paper for a teacher and fair judges, you may assume the reader is familiar with the broad theme of the subject area. In other words, *don't include everything you know or have learned about the subject*. It is the quality, not the quantity that counts. While you are researching, you will learn far more than you need to include in the paper. You will develop a sense of what you should and should not include. Keep in mind that your paper will include only what the audience needs to know to understand your project.

> **WINNING STRATEGY #2**
>
> For every bit of information you include in your paper, ask yourself: why is this interesting and what significance do these facts have to my project?

WHAT?

What might you want or need to know in order to write a paper and conduct an experiment? Before you begin researching, make a list of the questions that come to your mind about your project. Using the gerbil and maze project as an example, some of the questions the student might want to research are: What are gerbils? What do they eat? How intelligent are they? How long is their life span? What size are they? Is there a difference between male and female in their learning ability? What other sorts of experiments have been done on gerbils?

You can also add what sources you plan to check for the information. Would you look in an encyclopedia, a book about pets? Would you visit a pet store or talk to a veterinarian?

Researching requires a plan for carefully collecting and recording information so that you can refer back to it as you write your paper. There are three widely used methods.

- *Highlighting.* When you photocopy a magazine article or a book page, highlight the pertinent facts. You will include these pages in your reprints file (see box) later and the highlighting shows the judges exactly what interested you in the article or text.

- *Note-taking on index cards.* This is the method favored by most researchers because the information can be laid out in various orders while you are writing. That way it is easier to organize your thoughts and to be sure you've included every fact. The drawback to this method is working within the confines of the card.

- *Note-taking in your logbook.* This is helpful if you are a person who needs lots of space to

> **WINNING STRATEGY #3**
>
> Whenever possible, try to write the information in your own words, rather than using direct quotes. This can help you avoid plagiarism.

write. But, using the log can be a hassle because you have to flip through the pages when you are writing the paper. It is easy to miss some important facts this way. And, you cannot tear pages from the log and arrange them in the order in which you want to present the facts.

THE REPRINTS FILE

The reprints file is a binder, folder, or notebook in which you store all the photocopies of research articles or the actual articles, pamphlets, or printed material of background information. The articles may be placed in alphabetical order and it is helpful to judges if you put a copy of your bibliography in the front of the file to serve as a table of contents. If you are using a binder, place the articles in plastic protector sheets to keep them clean and neat.

NOTE-TAKING MADE SIMPLE

As you read your background sources, avoid the temptation to record everything from that source in one location, such as on one index card. Instead, divide your cards according to subject and label the top of the card with that subject title. Also, on the top of the card, write out the source information: The name of the author (last name first), the title of the book or article, the publisher, the place it was published (for books), the volume number (for magazines), and the date of publication. You will need this information when you put together the bibliography.

Below the title information, write the fact, quotation, or summary of information, and the page number. Paraphrasing while note-taking is the first step toward avoiding plagiarism. (See Chapter 8 for more on this subject.)

A sample note card for our "Can Gerbils Learn?" project might look like this:

Webster's New World Encyclopedia, Pocket ed., Prentice Hall, NY, 1993.

Gerbil

P. 341   member of Cricetidae family of rodents
           long back legs, hairy tails, from mouse to rat sized
           from Asia or Africa

Figure 4.1

When you are ready to write the paper, you can lay out all the cards, grouped according to topic. As you include each fact, you can check each card off with a pencil. At the end, you will know exactly what you included in the paper and where it came from. When it comes time to write the bibliography, arrange the cards in alphabetical order by the author's last name and you're all set.

Next, write an outline. An outline helps you organize the material in logical fashion. It also lets you decide what material isn't really relevant and can be withheld from the final paper. Your outline might be simply a list of the topics (use the subject headings of your note cards) or a more elaborate one with phrases and subtopics. The advantage of writing a more detailed outline is that you can then include those phrases in your paper and your paper will practically write itself.

OUTLINING MADE SIMPLE

Remember outlining? You start with "I" and then under that, an "A" and perhaps a "1." Get confused with what goes where? Don't worry about it. This outline is just for your use. The basic idea is to develop a theme phrase for each paragraph of your paper. That phrase is listed first, and under it, you can write other phrases you want to include to elaborate on the first phrase. Simple outlining doesn't include complete sentences, but just enough information to capture the idea.

Sample Outline

I. Gerbils
  A. What type of animal are they?
  B. Where do they come from?
  C. Why are they used for research projects?
  D. What do they like to eat?
II. Maze
  A. How to build?
  B. What might motivate a gerbil to run a maze?

Figure 4.2

WHERE?

Students often make the mistake of heading for the library or the Internet to begin their research before they make a plan. Believe it or not, you need to know what you are looking for *before* you go after it, or you can spend hours confused or distracted. Then equip yourself with either note cards or paper and plenty of change for the copy machine.

INSIDER'S TIP

Do not rely solely on the Internet for background information. Judges want to see a variety of types of sources. Information on the Internet can be inaccurate as it does not have to pass through the critical eyes of reviewers and editors. Always consider the source of the information. Is it authoritative or one person's opinion?

RESEARCH MADE SIMPLE

To start your research on the Internet, use any search vehicle, such as Alta Vista, Excite and Yahoo. You can type in the keyword "gerbil" and see what you get back, but you'll soon have more information than you have time to read. The Internet can be very helpful, but also overwhelming in the amount of information delivered to your computer. Try narrowing the search by using, "gerbil+life span," "gerbil+habitat," etc. Don't forget you can "bookmark" helpful articles to return to them later. Print the ones you think you might use so that you can add them to your reprints file. (See Appendix for more on online researching.)

The public library is an excellent source of different types of information. Some of the types of references available there are:

- Online catalog
- Encyclopedias
- Dictionaries
- Bibliographies
- Government documents
- Almanacs, Yearbooks, Annuals
- Directories
- Biographies
- Maps, Atlases
- Newspapers, Periodicals
- Indexes, Abstracts, Graduate Theses

Once again, be sure to consider the source. When dealing with crucial facts, compare the information in several sources to be sure it is accurate and up-to-date. When you find a pertinent book or magazine article, check the references or bibliography for other sources of information. From one source, you may be directed to a dozen other articles or books.

Every library has a reference librarian who can be immensely helpful to a serious student. Ask for help. If a reference isn't available at your local library, ask the librarian if an interlibrary loan can be arranged.

WHEN?

As we've said, the time to start planning for your research paper is as soon as you select a topic. But knowing when to stop researching is just as important as knowing when to start. Some students keep researching a subject forever and end up with enough material to write a book rather than a paper. They waste precious time and end up with too much information. Your paper must be concise and organized. If you find yourself going off in too many directions, refer back to your original list of questions to research.

HOW?

Beginning in the first paragraph, introduce your project. Each paragraph should contain a single idea. Remember your paper is not a series of quotations from the sources strung together. You need to include pertinent information, *in your own words,* and with some sense of flow so that each paragraph can stand independently, but is connected to the next.

> **WINNING STRATEGY #4**
>
> Follow the scientific method in organizing the information in your paper.

Use the scientific method again. Your first paragraph states your purpose, the question, and hypothesis. Then, focus on background information with a paragraph or two for each major topic. Next, list your procedure as a step-by-step recipe for the experimentation. Then, summarize your results.

Your teacher may want you to include your data, charts, graphs, and statistical analysis here. Ask. Some prefer that the paper be a narrative without interruption. Your final two paragraphs should be your conclusion: a summary of your findings and whether your work supported or disproved the hypothesis. The last paragraph might repeat the significance of the project and your plans, if any, for future study.

> **WINNING STRATEGY #5**
>
> The research paper is always written in third person. Don't write "I" did this or that, instead, refer to yourself as "the researcher," or "this researcher." You may want to do the same thing in your logbook to help you remember to use the third person.

INSIDER'S TIP

Always check your spelling. Use the spell-checker function of the word processing program, but do not depend on it. Common errors with spell-checker programs are synonyms such as "to," "two," and "too." The spell-checker will recognize them as spelled correctly, but they may not have been used correctly. A sloppy paper can make the difference between a first- and second-place finish.

FORMATTING YOUR PAPER MADE SIMPLE

The format (how the paper looks when typed up) may be determined by the teacher and you should receive certain guidelines, or you may refer to the *MLA Handbook for Writers of Research Papers* which can be found in any library. Some simple "rules" are:

- Use white 8½- by 11-inch paper (not notebook paper).

- Type it on a word processor or typewriter.

- Leave 1-inch margins on all sides, including top and bottom, and only type on one side of the paper.

- Double-space everything, including quotations, notes, and the bibliography.

- Use of a title page depends on your teacher's guidelines. If you are using a binder or some sort of cover for your paper, that can serve as the title page.

- Number the pages. (If you ever drop the paper and have to figure out what goes where you will appreciate having page numbers.) The number belongs in the upper right-hand corner.

- Bind it all together with a staple in the upper left-hand corner, a paper-clip, a report cover, or put it into a binder, depending on what your teacher requires. If you use a binder, you may wish to slide each page into a plastic sheet. This keeps the copy clean and makes it easier for judges to flip through your paper quickly.

- Use Times New Roman or Courier fonts, 12 point, for the text and avoid fancy fonts and italics as much as possible. Your goal is to look professional, neat, and conventional in your paper. Large print does not make up for a short paper; it makes the brevity more obvious.

- Unless your teacher requires a dedication or acknowledgment page, skip them. Professional researchers do not dedicate their paper to the parents, teacher, best friend, or person who helped them. (You can send them a personal thank-you note.)

Finish your paper by citing your references. You will need to use two different methods for this. First, cite the sources you directly quoted in the paper using parenthetical notation. (In other words, put the information inside parentheses.) This is known as *textual citation*; details of how to use textual citation are found at the end of Chapter 8. The second list of references is the *bibliography,* an alphabetical list of all the references you used. If you have written this information on your note cards, it is simple to stack them in alphabetic order and transfer the information to your paper. The format of the references and the bibliography differ slightly and you will find more information on these in Chapter 8.

INSIDER'S TIP

When you finish the paper, read it out loud. Does it sound right? Do the paragraphs flow together well and make sense? Have someone else read it also. Do you or the reader have any questions about the topic or project that weren't answered in the paper?

PUTTING IT TOGETHER ON ONE PAGE

The true test of your ability to use the writing skills covered in this chapter will come when you are called upon to write an abstract for your research project. The **abstract** is a concise summary of your research. It describes your experimental question, hypothesis, practical application, background, procedures, results, conclusions, and sources . . . in one page or less! The ISEF allows abstracts to be a *maximum* of 250 words. There isn't room to thank people here, either.

The abstract is usually the very last part of your research paper that you will write because it requires that you have results from the experiment and conclusions. The format of the paper must follow very strict guidelines which have been known to vary from year to year, so consult your teacher or supervisor for the current template.

Generally, the title of your project appears at the very top of the page and may be centered. Most science fairs ask that students not list identifying information, such as their name or school. The title alone will suffice. The body of the abstract follows (usually after four to six lines of empty space). The body should contain a statement or two of background mentioning the purpose or application of the research. Next the hypothesis is stated, fol-

---

INSIDER'S TIP

A smaller font, Times New Roman, size eleven, may be used for the abstract since you have a limited space and number of words to fit onto that single page.

---

lowed by a description of the experimental methods. Finally, you should summarize the results in a general way and report your conclusions.

After several more lines of space, you can list two or three of the most valuable reference sources in standard bibliographic format (see Chapter 8 for more information.)

WINNING # STRATEGY 6

Take special care to polish your abstract because it is often the first part of your project the judges see.

INSIDER'S TIP

Judges may ask about the references listed on the abstract. Be sure you have chosen the most important ones and you are familiar with them. You'll also want to vary the type of source listed —it is not a good idea to cite three Web sources or three books. Demonstrate that you are a well-rounded researcher who used several different reference tools in your information gathering.

WINNING STRATEGIES

1. The research paper is not simply a listing of sources. A good paper is focused and organized. Start thinking about how you'll organize your project before you even begin the research.

2. For every bit of information you include in your paper, ask yourself: why is this interesting and what significance do these facts have to my project?

3. Whenever possible, try to write the information in your own words, rather than using direct quotes. This can help you avoid plagiarism.

4. Follow the scientific method in organizing the information in your paper.

5. The research paper is always written in third person. Don't write "I" did this or that, instead, refer to yourself as "the researcher," or "this researcher." You may want to do the same thing in your logbook to help you remember to use the third person.

6. Take special care to polish your abstract because it is often the first part of your project the judges see.

5

Murphy's Law of Science Research

If Anything Can Go Wrong, It Will

Sam Student was testing the effects of ultraviolet radiation on two different kinds of microorganisms: paramecium and daphnia. Sam placed an order for these microorganisms with Acme Biological Supply Company two months before the school fair. However, within a week Acme contacted him to say they were all out of daphnia. They did, however, have plenty of amoebae. Sam did a bit of research and decided that amoebae would be a good substitution for the daphnia. So he changed his order, and headed back to the library to research the eating habits of amoebae.

A shipment arrived two weeks later and Sam got to work creating cultures. However, Christmas break fell right in the middle of when he'd planned to begin experimentation. His data collection method required taking samples, preparing slides, and taking population counts every third day using a microscope. Sam would have to begin after the holiday break. He arranged with his research teacher to leave the cultures in an environmentally controlled incubator and gave them enough food to last the week. Then, a power outage during the vacation caused the incubator to shut off. Sam returned to find all of his microorganism cultures dead. He had to place another order with the company and start all over again. The science fair was now less than three weeks away.

Do situations like Sam's really occur? Yes. The moral of Sam's story? Plan ahead. Way ahead.

TIME IS OF THE ESSENCE

A recent survey conducted among middle-school and high-school science research students asked, "What were some of the challenges that you faced in conducting your experiment?" Most students responded: "the time crunch." One student admitted that he didn't realize his "experimentation would take so long." Another said that she'd lost time while "waiting for supplies." One summed it best when he explained that the biggest problem of all was "getting the project done at the last minute!"

The majority of students have an entire school year (or more) to work on research, experimentation, data analysis, and preparing the presentation. So, why do students face a time crunch? There are many contributing factors. You may be involved in many activities at school and after school. Students who excel in science research tend to excel in other areas. If you are anything like the typical research student, you're probably struggling to juggle your Advanced Placement coursework, spending time with your boyfriend or girlfriend, playing in the school band, and working as a bagger at the local grocery in addition to doing a science fair project!

CREATING A TIMELINE

With so many factors both in and out of your control you need to establish a timeline for yourself. A timeline is simply a list of dates that are your targets for completing certain tasks. Your instructor may have already given you a schedule of deadlines. Aim ahead of those deadlines. You don't want to scramble at the last moment to get things turned in, especially if it's a situation where your grade is affected. If your instructor doesn't provide deadlines, make up your own. A reasonable timeline might look something like this:

Your Timeline

Month 1	Select topic, start logbook, begin research, apply for SRC approval
Month 2	Develop hypothesis, continue research, and start paper
Month 3	After approval, begin experimentation, note results in logbook
Month 4	Finish experimentation, complete paper, prepare backboard
Month 5	Do data analysis, print final copies of paper, abstract, practice presentation, science fair

Figure 5.1

This schedule can easily be adapted to your project and your instructor. But, if you find yourself in the middle of the third month and you've not received approval or begun researching the topic, you'll have to work very hard to catch up.

WINNING # 1 STRATEGY

Create a timeline for your project.

After you have developed a fairly concrete experimental plan (one that your teacher or supervisor has approved), sit down with a calendar. You'll need to consider the following questions in creating your timeline:

INSIDER'S TIP

Always allow extra time at the end of the timeline because that is when you have the greatest stress to complete everything. You can also use this time to make up for any time lost earlier due to unforeseen setbacks of one kind or another.

When is the science fair?

The first thing you need to consider in establishing your timeline is the date of the science fair itself. This might seem obvious, but you'd be surprised how much work students leave until the last moment. Plan to finish experimentation *at least* two weeks before the fair. This will give you time to apply statistical analysis to your results, create graphs and charts, formulate your conclusions, finish your backboard and final paper, and take care of a host of other last-minute details. Setting aside this time will enable you to avoid the challenge of "getting the project done at the last minute."

WINNING STRATEGY #2

Plan to finish your experimentation at least two weeks before the science fair.

How long will it take to get approval?

Every project requires approval, first from your teacher, then often from the Scientific Review Committee, a state-level review board that sets standards for projects and must approve them when chemicals, plants, animals, microorganisms, DNA, or certain procedures are used. Approval of experimental protocol can sometimes take weeks.

How long will it take to do the research?

If you chose a project with very specialized information, it may take longer for you to gather the background information to write your paper and develop your procedure.

How long will it take to obtain materials?

This is an especially important factor because you can't even begin the experiment without the supplies that you need. If you are ordering items from a biological supply company, how long will it take for them to arrive? What will you do if your order is out-of-stock, or back-ordered? Always have a backup plan. Research secondary sources for materials or supplies; use local sources whenever possible to save on shipping time. Determine alternate materials you could substitute if necessary. For example, if your experiment involves marigolds, could you use another flower instead? Could you substitute amoebae for paramecium if need be? One student needed vitamin C in solution and so she crushed tablets and added the powder to water.

However, the solution did not react properly. She switched to a powdered ascorbic acid which worked.

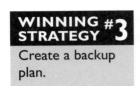

What about cost? Is there a limit to the budget for supplies? Be certain to talk to your teacher about the projected cost for your supplies. When one student realized the special glassware she needed would cost several hundred dollars, she asked people to save baby food jars for her and they were perfect for her procedure.

How long will an experimental trial take?

Allow yourself enough time to repeat your experiment completely in case all of your microorganisms die, your chemicals are mistakenly thrown away by the janitor, or the computer program you are creating crashes.

How many runs of the experiment will you need to get sufficient data for your conclusions? Can you run multiple trials simultaneously? Will your experimentation have different stages, with each dependent on the preceding trial? Determine these details before you begin experimentation.

Are there any holidays or other events that you need to consider?

Mark on your calendar the days that you will experiment and gather data. How will Saturdays and Sundays affect your plan? Are there any holidays, three-day weekends, or vacation breaks that you need to plan around? Will your school or laboratory site be made available to science research students so that you can take advantage of this time? Will the scientist you're working with be available when you need him or her? Discuss his or her schedule and availability in advance to prevent time conflicts. One science research teacher at a local junior high keeps the lab open to students over the winter holiday week and spring break. On any given day, ten to twenty students can be found working on their backboards, peering through microscopes, or analyzing data on the computers.

Consider your own personal and family schedules as well—are there any band competitions, drama conferences, or family trips that might interfere with your work on your project?

TIME MANAGEMENT TIPS

Time is a set quantity. There are 24 hours to a day, 168 hours in a week, and so on. You have no control over the quantity of time between now and the science fair, but you do have the ability to better manage the time you have. Effective time management can make your project go more smoothly. Here are some tips for time management:

- Know yourself. What other demands are there on your time and what are your priorities at this point in your life? (A priority is something requiring specific attention to which you want to give the most time, and consideration.) If science research is a priority, you may have to sacrifice some other things to make time for it in your schedule. Research has to be something that you do for yourself, not because a parent or teacher wants you to.

- Include science research in your daily schedule. Research cannot take up what's "left over" of your day. If you make a commitment, you have to stick with it even on the days you don't feel like going to the lab because your friends are going to the mall. If you make research a part of your daily schedule, it will be much more manageable and enjoyable. Working on your backboard or paper in smaller, daily segments will save you from having huge amounts of work to do right before the fair. Keep in mind that you will have time for everything else in a few months.

- Follow your plan. As someone once said, probably about a science project, you don't plan to fail, you fail to plan. Your timeline is your plan. Fill in the exact dates according to your instructor's schedule and your individual project. Give yourself plenty of time in each stage of the project in case something goes wrong. Remember to revise your timeline if there's a significant change in plans.

- Delete time killers from your life. Only you can decide what those are, but some suggestions: long telephone calls, television programs, video games, surfing the Web, "hanging out." You still need to have a social life, but you may need to put some activities on hold until the project is done.

- Don't get sidetracked. Avoid the temptation to research irrelevant material and broaden the experimentation. A simple project done thoroughly is far better than a complex one done poorly or so rushed that you cannot give each step the time it requires.

- Take careful notes while you are researching. Highlight important information in your reprints. Transfer any quotes that you want to include in your paper onto note cards. Be sure you write down the source exactly, so you don't waste precious time trying to find the same source again. Place your reprints in a binder so you have them all together for future reference. You can sort the reprints by subject or place them in alphabetical order by author's last name as the bibliography will list them.

- When you work with a computer, remember the cardinal rule: *back up everything frequently*. Every time you sit down at the keyboard, back up your work before you leave. This simple step will save you time and heartache if the computer crashes.

INSIDER'S TIP

Do not back up to a disk at school and take that disk home to your computer. No matter how careful you are, a computer virus can be transferred from one computer to another. One student brought a disk home to finish her paper two days before the fair and infected her home computer, destroying all Word files on the computer and the disk. If you *must* transfer work from one computer to another, always scan the disk for viruses first before opening the file. Be equally cautious opening an e-mail attachment or downloading files from the Internet.

BE PREPARED

Prepare for any emergency that might occur the day of the fair. Vandals almost destroyed one student's presentation by defacing the papers on her backboard. Fortunately, she had printed and brought with her an extra set of everything and could easily replace them.

Of course, no amount of planning and tools could help one student. She broke out with chicken pox the night before the fair. In science research, as in life, there will always be disasters that no amount of planning or preparation can account for. In those cases, you just have to grin and bear it!

> **WINNING STRATEGY #4**
>
> Prepare an emergency kit of tools and supplies you might need to make quick repairs of your backboard or display.

WINNING STRATEGIES

1. Create a timeline for your project.
2. Plan to finish your experimentation at least two weeks before the science fair.
3. Create a backup plan.
4. Prepare an emergency kit of tools and supplies you might need to make quick repairs of your backboard or display.

6

Safety First

Safety Guidelines for Experimentation

There can be no substitute for caution when working in a lab. For many students, the lab is a foreign environment with its own set of rules and those rules must be followed for your own safety as well as that of others working there. Learn the rules first. Your teacher or lab may have a different set of rules, but these are common ones.

LAB SAFETY RULES

1. Never eat or drink anything or store food in the lab. This includes chewing gum.

2. If you need to wear a lab coat or apron over your street clothing, don't wear it outside the lab.

3. Tie back long hair, roll up long sleeves, and wear close-toed shoes.

4. Report fires or personal injuries. Be sure the lab is equipped with a fire extinguisher and a first aid kit. Know where they are and whom to notify in case of trouble.

5. Wash hands thoroughly when you enter and before you leave the lab.

6. Dispose of waste in proper containers or according to school or lab policies. Never pour any chemicals down the sink without checking with the instructor first.

7. Assemble everything you will need ahead of time and keep everything within reach. By limiting the space in which you work, you will have less surface to clean before and after your work, and fewer steps to walk. It may also help you to be more safety-conscious.

CHEMICALS

Whenever you are experimenting with chemicals, it is important to understand how you should properly handle the chemical, how you must dispose of it, and what to do in case of emergency. Material Safety Data Sheets (MSDS) are invaluable. You can obtain these from your chemical supplier or a Merck Index.

> **INSIDER'S TIP**
>
> Add the MSDS sheet to your reprints file. A judge may want to know you have one and ask to see it.

Discuss safety and disposal with your teacher or mentor *before* you begin experimentation. Consider questions like:

- Does the chemical require using heavy gloves?
- Do I need to be under a fume hood when pouring it?

> **WINNING STRATEGY #1**
>
> Take responsibility for understanding the safety, disposal, and emergency precautions for every chemical you are using in your experimentation.

- Does the chemical need to be diluted before disposal or stabilized with another agent? What should I do if I get it on my skin or in my eyes?
- What do I need to know about this chemical before I handle it?

Consider different scenarios and rehearse exactly how you would respond if something were to go wrong. The lab should be equipped with a safety station; be sure you know where it is and how to use it.

LABS ARE DANGEROUS PLACES

Aside from chemicals, there are other dangers in the lab. Some projects require the use of electricity for lights, microscope, and electrical tools. Commonsense rules apply here:

- Never stretch an electrical cord across a walkway.
- Never place a cord near or in water.
- Keep flammable objects away from sources of heat.
- Any electrical apparatus that operates with 115-volt current should be constructed in accordance with the National Electrical Code (NEC.) When in doubt, contact an electrician.
- Most experiments can be performed using a 6- or 12-volt electrical source. These are much safer and their use should be considered when doing a project.

WHAT'S GREEN, GLOWS IN THE DARK, AND IS GROWING ON MY PROJECT?

Many students find working with microorganisms to be an exciting aspect of science research. Heather will never forget her seventh grade experiment involving caloric intake and life span in paramecium. The first time she peeked under the microscope and focused on the paramecium moving about on the slide, she was entranced. Working with microorganisms like bacteria, viruses, molds, yeast, or spores can, however, be tricky, as Heather found when she accidentally contaminated her cultures with daphnia, another microorganism that she was using. The daphnia ate all of her paramecium.

When working with microorganisms, always purchase pure cultures from reputable supply companies. Students should *never* use cultures taken directly or indirectly from humans or other warm-blooded animals because of the danger that unknown viruses or other disease-causing agents may be present. Experiments involving recombinant DNA technology must comply with the National Institutes of Health guidelines unless the project is limited to a kit obtained from a biological supply house.

> **WINNING STRATEGY #2**
>
> Practice handling dishes, pipettes, swabs, or test tubes so that you feel less awkward when it comes to working with an actual culture medium. Have someone watch you to be sure you don't accidentally contaminate what you are working with.

STERILE TECHNIQUE

Inexperienced researchers often find accidental contamination to be a problem. The solution is to learn how to use sterile technique and use it every time you handle cultures or perform an experiment requiring the avoidance of contamination.

Sterile technique refers to precautions taken to prevent contamination with other microorganisms. Sterilizing usually involves using high temperatures under pressure (such as an autoclave) to kill all microorganisms present. Disinfecting refers to the use of chemical agents, such as alcohol, for the same purpose. Don't be intimidated; sterile technique, like many aspects of your work, simply requires practice and attention to detail.

INSIDER'S TIP

In addition to the MSDS sheets for chemicals used in your experiment, keep all of the paperwork from the supply house for any microorganisms used. You need to have available at the fair a copy of approval from the Scientific Review Committee (SRC) for work with humans, animals, pathogenic agents, controlled substances, recombinant DNA, and human or animal tissue.

STERILIZATION

An autoclave or pressure cooker uses moist heat to sterilize materials. At a pressure of 15 psi above atmospheric pressure, water reaches a temperature of 1210°C before it boils. Fifteen minutes under these conditions will sterilize most materials.

THE BASICS OF STERILE TECHNIQUE

1. Everything you touch or use, including your own hands, must be clean. Wash hands thoroughly, with special attention to your fingernails.

2. Be sure to remove all rings and bracelets and if you have long hair, tie it back.

3. As you work, avoid talking, chewing gum, singing, whistling, coughing, sneezing, or any activity in which you might breathe on a culture, solution, or medium. Keep air turbulence to a minimum.

4. The most common source of contamination is mold-laden dust. Clean your work surface with an antiseptic or 70 percent alcohol. Swab the exterior of any glassware as well.

5. Obtain all of your equipment and materials in advance and set up your work area so that your movement is minimized. Try to avoid reaching over one utensil to get another.

6. Always keep your eyes on whatever you are handling and keep whatever you are not using covered.

7. When opening a sterile flask, jar, or bottle, tilt it slightly so that spores in the air do not land and settle inside. Place screw caps with the open side down on a clean swabbed surface so that air doesn't touch exposed surfaces that may come in contact with the medium.

8. Do not touch the outside of the jar, flask, or petri dish with a sterile pipette, syringe, or swab. As much as possible, keep petri dishes covered and always hold the lid so that air cannot settle spores on top of the medium or on the inner surface of the lid.

9. Sterilize instruments with flame or in an autoclave, or soak them in 70 or 95 percent alcohol. Always shake off the excess alcohol before using the instrument. If you accidentally touch something with a sterile instrument, it must be re-sterilized before you can use it again.

10. When you are done working, repeat the same cleaning process by wiping down the work area with alcohol and washing your hands thoroughly.

WINNING STRATEGY #3

If you are using an autoclave or pressure cooker, you will need to know the temperature, time, and pressure and record this in your log.

Dry heat may also be used on materials such as glass and metal. In an oven, the temperature must reach 1600°C for at least two hours. Most kitchen oven dials reflect Fahrenheit temperatures. Use a Centigrade thermometer to register internal oven temperature. You may need to allow for overnight cooling if you use an oven.

The flame of a glass burner also sterilizes and is handy to use when working with small metal items and utensils such as loops. Working with an open flame is always hazardous and requires extra caution.

Alcohol, either 70 or 95 percent, is an effective and

convenient sterilizing agent for work surfaces. Allow it to evaporate before you begin working. Never put alcohol near an open flame.

If sterile water is needed, place the water in a loosely covered container and set the container in a pan of boiling water for 15 minutes. After the water cools, you can tighten the lid on the container to maintain the water's sterility. Some bacterial and fungal spores can survive in exposure to 121°C for 15 minutes, however, for all practical purposes, this time and temperature are considered acceptable to sterilize liquids.

BETTER SAFE THAN SORRY

These guidelines for lab safety and sterile technique may seem cumbersome and overly cautious. However, they are designed to protect you and those around you. Following rules for lab safety and sterility will mean that you don't have to redo results lost to contamination or carelessness. And, after a little bit of practice, you'll be surprised by how easy these ounces of prevention are to use!

WINNING STRATEGIES

1. Take responsibility for understanding the safety, disposal, and emergency precautions for every chemical you are using in your experimentation.

2. Practice handling dishes, pipettes, swabs, or test tubes so that you feel less awkward when it comes to working with an actual culture medium. Have someone watch you to be sure you don't accidentally contaminate what you are working with.

3. If you are using an autoclave or pressure cooker, you will need to know the temperature, time, and pressure and record this in your log.

7

Data, Not Just a *Star Trek* Character

How to Interpret and Display Data

As you proudly flip through the rows and columns of numbers neatly recorded in your logbook, you may be thinking, "Finally! I'm finished." However, now it's time to trade in that lab coat for a calculator, because the data analysis is just starting! Those pages and pages of numbers in your logbook are **raw data.** While they contain a lot of information, the numbers by themselves are not very meaningful to others.

Once you've completed the experimentation phase of your project and obtained raw data you need to work with the information to make it understandable to the scientific community. This chapter examines basic concepts of statistical analysis. **Statistics** refers to the gathering, display, and summary of raw data (such as a list of numbers) to gain meaningful information and to communicate your findings to others.

The use of statistics allows you to note patterns and trends in your data. It shows whether your results stem from a cause (such as one experimental variable) or merely from chance. In other words, analysis allows you to examine the cause-effect relationship that your hypothesis implies.

MAKING A DATA TABLE

The rows of numbers in your logbook represent a series of observations that you've made in the course of your data collection. You may have hundreds of columns of observations. The most basic level of data "treatment" is to organize your observations into a table. What might this look like?

Let's take a hypothetical example. Suppose you studied the effects of different carbon dioxide (CO_2) levels on bean plants. You had a control group that you exposed to normal atmospheric amounts of CO_2, or room air. You also had three variable groups, and the plants in those groups were exposed to 5 percent, 10 percent, and 20 percent greater concentrations of CO_2 than normal room air. Each group contained six plants. You recorded the growth of the control group and variable groups each day for a certain period of time. The measurements for a specific day are called an **array,** or data table.

A data table for the *control group only* for Day 12 (you would have a separate table for each group and for the days on which you measured the plants) might look like this:

Observation	1	2	3	4	5	6
Data Value (cm)	12	14	14.5	11	14	13

Table 7.1

How can you describe this table in a general way, instead of having to deal with six different measurements for this one group? Let's designate n to represent the number of observations made (or the number of plants you measured). Represent each value (measurement) observed as: $x_1, x_2, x_3, x_4 \ldots x_n$ The data table would then look like this:

Observation	1	2	3	4	...	n
Data Value	x_1	x_2	x_3	x_4	...	x_n

Table 7.2

Pairing observation with value is the simplest way to organize your data.

MEAN, MEDIAN, AND MODE: THE "THREE MUSKETEERS" OF STATISTICS

Let's continue with the hypothetical example of the bean plants. The table describes the heights of each individual plant in your control group. You probably have one or two plants that aren't doing as well as the others, and one plant that is growing much faster than the others. The reason you have used six plants in each group is to account for such differences in individual growing patterns. You need a way to convert the values of all six plants into one number. You need one value that will represent all of the data values.

In statistical analysis, there are three common methods to determine what is known as **typical values** for data: mean, median, and mode.

The most common typical value used is the mean. You have heard the term "average" before in math, but may not be familiar with its technical counterpart. The **mean** is the same as the average of the data, or the sum of a set of figures divided by the number of figures. The mean is represented by the symbol: $\bar{x}$. Refer back to Table 7.2 and you'll recall that we chose n to represent the number of observations made. Data values are represented by $x_1, x_2, x_3,$ and so forth. The formula for determining the mean is:

$$\bar{x} = (x_1 + x_2 + x_3 + x_4 + \ldots x_n)/n$$

Or, as in the case of the bean plant example:

$$\bar{x} = (12 + 14 + 14.5 + 11 + 14 + 13)/6$$

Taking it a further step:

13.08 cm (rounded to the nearest hundredth)

Another useful statistic is the **median,** or the midpoint of the data. To determine the median, sort the data from smallest to largest value. The sample plant data set

{12, 14, 14.5, 11, 14, 13} becomes: {11, 12, 13, 14, 14, 14.5}

The median is the halfway point—half of the values are above it and half below it. In the case of an odd number of data points (where n is odd), the median is the data value in the middle of the array. Were n equal to 11, you would select the sixth data point or value. In the case of an even number, such as in our example, the median is the average of the two points closest to the middle. In this particular case, the two values closest to the middle are the third and fourth. To calculate the median: (13 + 14)/2 = 13.5.

Lastly, the **mode** is used to indicate the values that occur most frequently. In our example, the value 14 occurs twice. All other values occur only once, therefore 14 is the mode. It is possible to have more than one mode in a data set.

INSIDER'S TIP

Of these "Three Musketeers," you'll probably use the mean calculation most often. It conveys the most basic information about the data. The mean is also important because it is used in determining the standard deviation (discussed later in this chapter).

WOULD YOU LIKE THAT IN A PIE, BAR, OR LINE?

A **graph** is a visual representation of your data. Like a table, it allows you to display data in a way that will be meaningful to observers. The visual aspect of a graph, however, makes it easier for others to see your results at a glance. There are many different kinds of graphs, and each is used to display very specific aspects of the data. Your choice of graphs must be as logical as your use of scientific method. A judge should be able to look at a graph and understand it with a minimum of examination. The three most common types of graphs are pie charts, bar graphs, and line graphs.

> **WINNING #2 STRATEGY**
> *Never* make a graph just for the sake of making a graph. Think carefully about what kind of graphs would best present your data.

Pie charts

A *pie chart* is circular and is used to represent the total amount of something divided into sections by percentage. The sections look like slices of a pie and the total percentages must equal 100.

For an appropriate example of when to use a pie chart, let's assume you are studying different diagnostic methods for skin cancer. Your sample size is fifty patients and the cancers are graded from A to E. You studied two diagnostic methods: microscopic evaluation of tissue and DNA extraction and assessment. Your results are as follows:

Diagnostic	Grade A	Grade B	Grade C	Grade D	Grade E
Tissue	6 patients	27 patients	12 patients	3 patients	2 patients
DNA	4 patients	15 patients	23 patients	5 patients	3 patients

Table 7.3

Nothing has been done to the data, other than recording it in a visually attractive and easy-to-read way. Note the title. It is brief, but accurately describes the contents of the table. This is acceptable for your paper or backboard display. You may even embellish it to make it easier to read at a distance by using shading on every other line, capitalizing all the letters, or using a bold font and larger size.

However, a judge might want to know the percentage of patients who were diagnosed with Grade A skin cancer using a microscope verses the percentage when DNA analysis was used. Two pie charts will demonstrate this comparison dramatically.

> **WINNING #3 STRATEGY**
> Always label graphs clearly with a descriptive title and accurate axes.

A comparison of different cancer diagnostic methods.

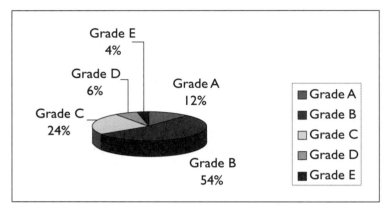

Figure 7.1   % Patients Diagnosed by Tissue

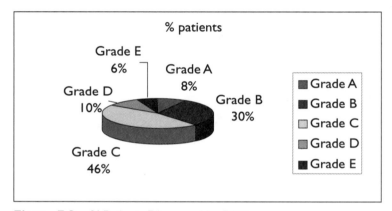

Figure 7.2   % Patients Diagnosed by DNA

Bar graphs

Bar graphs are used to demonstrate differences in frequency. The vertical axis (up and down on the left side) generally shows frequency expressed in number value, while the horizontal axis (left to right along the bottom of the graph) reflects the items being compared.

As an example, let's return to the bean plant experiment. If you wanted to compare the heights of the plants within each group on any given day, your data table might look like this:

Carbon Dioxide	Control	5% Greater	10% Greater	20% Greater
Average Plant Height (cm)	10.4	12.3	13.0	8.2

Table 7.4

A bar graph of this data would look like this:

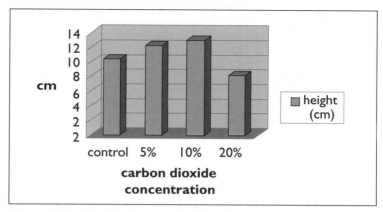

Figure 7.3 Graph of average height of plants, Day 9.

WINNING STRATEGY #4

When comparing different bar graphs make certain that the values on the vertical axes are the same. In other words, if you have used a spread of measurements with each point 2 cm greater than the last one, be sure every graph uses the same measurements. You would not want to use one graph with 2, 4, 6, 8, 10 cm, and the next graph with 5, 10 cm. Never mix centimeter measurements with inch measurements.

Line graphs

Changes or trends over time are depicted using *line graphs*. The bar graph above showed plant height on one given day. If you wanted to display growth of the plants over time, a line graph would be more appropriate. The data table might look like this:

Carbon Dioxide	Control	5% Greater	10% Greater	20% Greater
Day 0	0 cm	0 cm	0 cm	0 cm
Day 3	2.6	3.4	4.1	1.2
Day 6	6.5	8.3	10.2	5.4
Day 9	10.4	12.3	13.0	8.2
Day 12	11.0	12.5	13.2	9.0

Table 7.5

And the corresponding line graph like this:

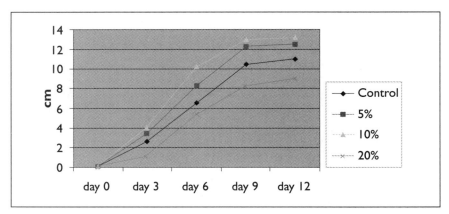

Figure 7.4   Line graph showing average growth of plants in different levels of CO_2.

Computer programs make graphing easy and you can be as fancy as you want to be. However, it is important that you are certain you understand different kinds of graphs and how each should be used. Your data display should always enhance and never detract from your presentation.

It is important to keep in mind the very different functions of pie, bar, and line graphs. The most common mistake that students make is choosing the wrong graph to represent their data. For example, see the graph below:

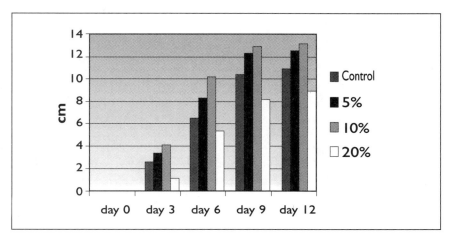

Figure 7.5   Bar graph showing average growth of plants in different levels of CO_2.

Remember the plants and carbon dioxide project? This graph of the data doesn't work, because it is supposed to reflect growth over time. You'll remember from our discussion of different types of graphs that a bar graph demonstrates change in frequency. A line graph would be a more appropriate choice.

OTHER COMMON GRAPHING MISTAKES

- Using measurements with a spread that is too small or too large.
- Mixing centimeters with inches, or cubic centimeters with ounces.
- Being inconsistent from one graph to the next.
- Using neon colors or colors that are too close to be distinguished from each other.
- Making or displaying too many graphs.
- Substituting flashy graphs for substance. Graphs do not make up for lack of data.

As your understanding of statistics grows, you'll be expected to use more than simple tables and graphs to explain and display your data.

MEASURING THE RANGE OF YOUR RESULTS

When doing an experiment over and over, you will find a range of results. If you consider your own observation of the natural world, this makes sense. Within the control group of bean plants, for example, you would not anticipate each plant to be *exactly* the same height, though growing conditions are the same. You'd expect to find some plants that are a little taller, some a little shorter. You would, however, expect them to be around the same height.

Scientists examine this common range of variation by using **standard deviation.** Standard deviation measures the spread of the data from the mean, or average. It also defines the range of results that can be attributed to normal variation. If results show too much variation, they may not be reliable or reproducible by another scientist.

There are computer programs and spread sheets that will calculate standard deviation for you. You should still understand what this calculation is and how it is determined.

Standard deviation is very good for summarizing data that is fairly symmetrical and "normally distributed," or mound-shaped (see figure below). The data set should also be large (approximately twenty observations or more) to be considered reliable.

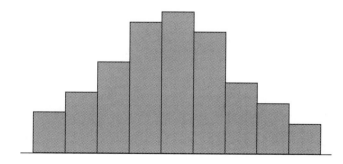

Figure 7.6
Mound-shaped representation of standard deviation.

For these kinds of data sets, there is a known relationship between the percentage of the data that fall within certain standard deviations from the mean. Approximately 68 percent of the data is within one standard deviation from the mean and 95 percent falls within two standard deviations from the mean. This is known as a 95 percent **confidence interval** for the sample.

What about data that is between one and two standard deviations from the average? What about data that is not "normally" distributed? There are several good books devoted solely to these topics and other aspects of statistics. Several are mentioned in the back of this book. Happy reading!

WINNING STRATEGY #5

Never apply a statistical test, such as standard deviation, to your data just for the sake of applying a test. You should always understand *why* you're using a certain test or kind of analysis, and *how* the test works.

WINNING STRATEGIES

1. Be certain to organize your data collection in your logbook neatly and clearly label information such as the date, whether it is the control or variable group, type of measurement (meters or centimeters for example), etc.

2. *Never* make a graph just for the sake of making a graph. Think carefully about what kind of graphs would best present your data.

3. Always label graphs clearly with a descriptive title and accurate axes.

4. When comparing different bar graphs make certain that the values on the vertical axes are the same. In other words, if you have used a spread of measurements with each point 2 cm greater than the last one, be sure every graph uses the same measurements. You would not want to use one graph with 2, 4, 6, 8, 10 cm, and the next graph with 5, 10 cm. Never mix centimeter measurements with inch measurements.

5. Never apply a statistical test, such as standard deviation, to your data just for the sake of applying a test. You should always understand *why* you're using a certain test or kind of analysis, and *how* the test works.

8

Misteaks, Mistaxe, Mistackes, Mistakes

Sweating the Small Stuff

The day of the fair has finally arrived and you are nervously awaiting your first judge of the morning. You have a pointer in hand, your backboard is perfect, you've made copies of your abstract to give to the judges. While you wait, you quickly scan over a copy and notice not one, but two typos!

The day of the fair is not the time to catch mistakes in your final paper or notebooks, on your backboard, or in your handouts. Simple, common errors can make the difference between a first place–winning project and a lower place, and these types of mistakes are preventable and fixable, until you are face-to-face with the judges, that is!

CATCHING SPELLING AND GRAMMATICAL ERRORS

Always use the spell-checker function of your word processing program. Never trust your own spelling, even if you won the eighth grade spelling bee. You may have many technical or scientific terms in your research paper that the computer will stumble over, but you can add them to the computer's vocabulary. The spell-checker won't catch everything, however.

Keep in mind as you proofread that many words have multiple correct spellings while meanings differ, such as "two" and "too" or "their" and "there." Spell-checkers also only find words that are incorrectly spelled. Therefore, if you typed "you" instead of "your," the spell-checker won't find it and you'll have an error. After you use the spell-checker function, proofread everything yourself. Then, have at least two people read your paper and every document on your backboard.

> **WINNING STRATEGY #1**
>
> One way to catch errors in your paper is to read it aloud. It is often easier to hear a mistake than to see it.

COMMON SPELLING AND GRAMMATICAL ERRORS

Affect/Effect.

The most common error made by science research students involves the difference between "affect" and "effect." "Affect," when used as a verb, means "to produce a change;" "effect" is always a noun and describes the result of a change. For example, the title of your project might be, "A Study of the Effects of Smoking on Rats," or you might ask the question, "Are Rats Affected by Smoking?"

Single/Plural.

Always use the plural form of a verb with a plural noun and the singular form of a verb following a singular noun. Now, the tricky part: in technical writing, "data" is a plural noun, so it takes the plural form of the verb. (In more casual writing, you will see it with a singular verb as this is becoming more acceptable, but for your paper and your backboard, use plural verbs with the word "data.") Bacteria is another word that is plural, however, rarely does anyone use the singular "bacterium" and, therefore, it is becoming more acceptable to follow "bacteria" with a singular verb. Examples: "The data show that the hypothesis was correct." "Bacteria thrive on sugar." Other tricky plurals include: fungi, larvae, criteria, hypotheses, phenomena, and stimuli.

"None" is always a single noun, requiring a singular verb, because it refers to "not one." Ignore the phrase following it when determining the verb. For example: "None of the seniors wants to win." (While the sentiment is incorrect, the grammar is fine.)

Another common error occurs with possession. If the noun is singular, an adjective used to describe possession must also be singular. For example, "The researcher must write everything in his own words," not, "in their own words. You may be tempted to use "his/her" or "his or her," to be politically correct. In scientific writing, "his" is considered acceptable unless you have made it clear that the subject is a female.

Tense.

Use verb tense consistently throughout a paragraph in your paper. (This is a good rule for all writing, not just science research.) For example, the following is incorrect, "Dr. Jones discovered the ploidy of the DNA of lung cancer and he writes . . ." The second verb "writes" should be in the past tense. It should read, "Dr. Jones discovered the ploidy of the DNA of lung cancer and he wrote . . ."

Nouns as verbs.

Avoid the temptation to use a noun as a verb, until it comes into general use by society. Common examples include "modem" and "e-mail." Although I may say "I e-mailed you today," the correct sentence should be "I sent you an e-mail message." (Also a no-no, "I modemed you an e-mail.")

WHERE IT'S OK TO MAKE MISTAKES

Your logbook need not be so perfect, so don't worry about spelling and grammatical errors there. (Just be sure to fix the errors before transferring them to your paper or backboard.) Since the logbook contains a day-by-day record of what you did, it should not look as though you wrote it the night before the fair. It should be *handwritten* in pen, not pencil, and never copied. Judges appreciate clear and legible handwriting, however, if yours is not, consider printing.

> ### INSIDER'S TIP
>
> The only time a logbook can be copied is when you have spilled something on it or when the original has been lost in a flood, fire, or tornado. Judges understand natural disasters. The logbook-eating dog never works as an excuse.

Although the logbook doesn't have to be super neat, avoid including in it daily activities not pertinent to your project. The logbook is not the place to record a friend's phone number so that you can call her later. You do not need to describe the outfit you have chosen to wear for the fair. You do not need to write what you had for lunch the day you conducted experiments, unless that was part of the experimentation. And, be careful about references to your teacher. They do read logbooks and so do judges!

PREVENTING PLAGIARISM

You may have been warned to avoid plagiarism in writing a school paper. What exactly does this mean? To plagiarize, according to *The American Heritage Dictionary,* is to "use the ideas or writings of another and pass them off as one's own." The academic community takes plagiarism very seriously because it represents not only laziness but also dishonesty.

What exactly constitutes plagiarism? Obviously, copying entire pages, paragraphs, and sentences from a source without giving credit is wrong. On the other hand, no one has a copyright on the entire English language and you needn't place quotation marks around every word or thought in your paper.

When is it vital to name your source and when is it unnecessary? One teacher told his students that a good rule of thumb was whether or not the fact was common knowledge. If you didn't know it before you started your research, it needs to be credited to a bibliographic source. In other words, the statement that "the sun sets in the West" does not need to be attributed to a source, whereas a statistic about the temperature of the sun's core does.

The best way to avoid plagiarism is by developing good habits during the information gathering stage. Read a paragraph or two and then *close the book* to write your own thoughts about the subject, what you remember, and how it may relate to your research. When doing research on the Internet, move away from the computer screen to jot down your notes. If you find a distinctive phrase or statistic you want to quote word-for-word, be certain to indicate that on your note card. Develop your own system to denote these quotes, and (as always) record the sources, including the page number.

Remember that changing a few words or the word order or sentence order is not enough to avoid plagiarism, even if you mix in statements of your own. This "patchwork plagiarism" still misrepresents ideas as being yours, when they are, in fact, not.

> **WINNING STRATEGY #2**
>
> To avoid plagiarism, close the book or move away from the computer you are using, then write down notes, in your own words, on what you have just read.

GIVING CREDIT WHERE CREDIT IS DUE

Now that you understand the necessity of citing sources, what is the proper format for doing so? Why have we included this section in a chapter about mistakes? Many students either apply the rules of citation format inconsistently or not at all.

According to *Technical Communications* (St. Martin's Press, 1998), there are three reasons for documenting your sources. Proper citation:

- Acknowledges your debt to those sources and prevents plagiarism.

- Establishes your credibility and places your work within the context of your particular field of research.

- Allows others to find sources to learn more information about the subject.

What kind of information should be cited? Any quotation or statistic, any paraphrased information (unless it is common knowledge), and graphics or charts taken from another source. There are two kinds of citation your paper should contain: parenthetical notation and a bibliography. There are two major formats used in the academic community: the American Psychological Association (APA) system and the Modern Language Association (MLA) system. Examples shown in this chapter will use the MLA system (*The Modern Language Association Handbook for Writers of Research Papers,* 4th ed.) Check with your teacher as to which format he or she requires. Our discussion will not be completely comprehensive and you may find it a wise investment to purchase a copy of the manual for the particular style required. You will use it later in life, as well.

> **WINNING STRATEGY #3**
>
> Knowing what to cite and using proper citation format are important aspects of documenting your project.

Textual citation (MLA format)

This type of citation is a parenthetical notation (enclosed in parentheses) that directly follows the material being cited. It includes the author's last name and the page number(s) in the source that contains that information.

Example: Individuals who consistently exercised thirty minutes a day three times a week demonstrated less susceptibility to the common cold. (Tyler 138)

If you incorporate the author's name in the preceding sentence, it is not necessary to include it at the end. The page number(s) alone is sufficient.

Example: Tyler noted that individuals who consistently exercised thirty minutes a day three times a week demonstrated less susceptibility to the common cold. (138)

When referring to the entire book or document and not particular pages, obviously you wouldn't need to include page numbers. You can also refer to two or more sources in one parenthetical citation. Multiple sources are separated by a comma.

Example: Individuals who consistently exercised thirty minutes a day three times a week demonstrated less susceptibility to the common cold. (Tyler 138, Hackney 152)

If you use several sources by the same author, add an abbreviated form of the title to the notation to clarify, such as (Tyler, "Exercise and Health") or (Tyler, "Immunity.") For a source written by two or three authors, include all names. When there are more than three, you can list the first author followed by "et al."

When do you underline a source and when do you enclose it in quotation marks? Book titles are underlined, or may be italicized if the italics font is readable. Magazines articles or Internet article titles are placed inside quotation marks. For more specific instructions for other kinds of sources, see *The Modern Language Association Handbook for Writers of Research Papers* (Modern Language Association of America, 1995).

THE BIBLIOGRAPHY

This list appears at the end of your paper and includes all of the information others will need to find the sources that you used. Only include sources you actually *used* in your research that contributed something to your paper. Do not list any and every reference related to your topic in order to lengthen your bibliography.

Alphabetize the sources in the bibliography by the author's last name. If the publication was published by an organization, rather than a single author, use the first significant word in that organization's name. (For example, The American Heart Association would be listed under "A.") Indent the second line of the citation and any following lines a ½ inch. Leave one space between each part of the entry and one after each comma and colon. The following are examples for commonly used sources:

Book by one author

> Rosenbaum, Anthony. *Environmental Science*. New York: Prentice Hall, 1994.

The author's full name is stated, last name first. The title of the book is italicized or underlined and all important words are capitalized. Next the place of publication: publisher, and date are listed.

Book by two authors or more

> Smith, Michael, and Maria Rodriguez. *Programming in C++*. New York: IEEE, 1999.

In this case only the first author's name is listed in reverse order. A comma separates the names. For a book by four or more authors, state all of the names or use the first author's name followed by a comma and "et al."

Multiple works by the same author

> Burkholder, Kenneth. *Lichens*. London: Oxford University Press, 1997.
> ————. *Mosses and Ferns*. Los Angeles: UCLA Press, 1999.

For subsequent entries use three hyphens and a period. Within that author's entries, alphabetize by the title of the work.

Book published by an organization

In this case, treat the organization title as you would the name of the author.

> Environmental Protection Agency. *Lead Poisoning and You*. Publication 118–43. Washington, D.C: Liberty, 1998.

Magazine article

> Webster, David. "Greenhouse Gases and Global Warming." *Sierra* 11 Nov. 1997: 68–71.

The title of the article appears in quotation marks. Abbreviate months (except for May, June, and July) using the first three letters of the month. If an article has no author, alphabetize it by the first significant word in the title.

Newspaper article

> Cheng, Xiao-Yeh. "New Food-Born Bacteria Risks." *The New York Post* 8 May 2000, morning edition: 2A.

If the newspaper has more than one edition, include the edition in which the article appeared.

Personal interview

> Dr. Charles E. Regan, Director of the Claude Pepper Institute of Geriatrics. Personal Interview. 20 Oct. 1999.

State the name of the subject and any brief credentials and the date the interview took place.

World Wide Web site

The citations for web sites are based on the styles used in *Online!: A Reference Guide to Using Internet Sources* by Andrew Harnack and Eugene Kleppinger (St. Martin's Press, 1997.) For more detailed instruction on citing other online communications in a manner consistent with the MLA site, consult that book.

> Jackson, Tyler. "Internet Resources for Mathematicians." *Mathematics.* 1999. www.mathworks.com.html (18 Dec. 1999).

As in the above example, list the author of the web site or page, followed by the name of the page. Next comes the name of the site, date of last revision, the URL or address of the site, and date that you viewed the site.

There are, of course, many different types of sources you may need to cite: a lecture that you attended, a quotation of a quotation, an e-mail message, or an article included in a book, to name a few. You may want to invest in a copy of the style guide of your choice, or at the very least, check a copy out from your local library.

INSIDER'S TIP

Your paper can make or break your entire project. When the judges are trying to decide between two excellent projects, they will look at the paper, logbooks, and display for mistakes in grammar, spelling, and writing. Extra attention here can pay off.

WINNING STRATEGIES

1. One way to catch errors in your paper is to read it aloud. It is often easier to hear a mistake than to see it.

2. To avoid plagiarism, close the book or move away from the computer you are using, then write down notes, in your own words, on what you have just read.

3. Knowing what to cite and using proper citation format are important aspects of documenting your project.

9

You Only Have One Chance to Make a First Impression

Your Backboard

Your backboard is a billboard. It advertises your product, which, in this case, is your science fair project. Consider roadside signs for just a moment. What are the characteristics of an effective billboard? It is usually:

- Easy to read and understand, even at a distance.
- Attractive and eye-catching.
- Original, standing apart from the rest.

Figure 9.1
Original, eye-catching backboard.

Your backboard should show your process of experimentation: what you've done, how you did it, what you've learned. The display illustrates every aspect of the scientific method and includes not only your backboard, but also your logbook, paper, reprint file, abstract, and whatever forms the fair or your project required. It may include a computer, video, machinery used during experimentation, or models. For safety reasons, food, liquids, chemicals, plants, bacteria, viruses, or animals are generally not allowed.

The backboard is the centerpiece of the display. Its size will be determined by the fair and guidelines should be available. Be sure to follow these rules exactly or your project may be disqualified if it is oversized. Your backboard must be freestanding and most students find a three-sided board more effective and more stable than an easel-type display.

ASSEMBLY REQUIRED

First, check with your teacher to see if the school provides boards. If not, you may purchase a cardboard display or build a more sturdy, reusable backboard. Plywood, pressed board, or foam-core poster board are the most commonly used materials. There is, however, a lot of room for creativity. One student, whose project was about composting, used wood fencing as the backbone of her backboard. Another student emphasized his study of milk spoilage by covering his board in black and white fabric reminiscent of cows. The three-panel board allows you to organize the display, including graphs, photographs or drawings, and each element of the project.

Our favorite board is one made from plywood because it travels well, lasts for many years, and looks professional. However, it is heavy and cumbersome to store and move. A wooden board has the strength to support a separate title board that can fit across the top, giving stability and extra display space. If you use a separate title board attached to your backboard the entire unit must fit within the space requirements of the fair.

Building a board doesn't take a woodshop and special tools. The lumber yard may be willing to cut the wood to your specifications for free or for a small charge. A hand drill and screwdriver is all you need for the hinges to attach the side panels to the back and, perhaps, some hardware to attach the title across the top, if you are using a separate title board.

A wooden backboard can be painted, but it would require a new coat or two of paint every year to keep it looking fresh. One industrious and artistic student actually chose to paint a lake scene onto her backboard. She was studying fish species and in her case the painting did not detract from, but added to her display. If you choose to express yourself artistically with your backboard, make certain it will enhance your display.

Many students choose to cover their plywood backboards with felt for a professional, finished look. About 10 yards of 60-inch-wide felt is inexpensive and more than enough to cover the largest plywood board. Felt also comes in many colors; stick with a dark color that won't show dirt. A staple

Figure 9.2
A wood fence became the backboard for a project about composting.

gun can be used to apply the felt. You don't need to apply felt to the back of the board, just wrap it neatly over the edges and staple in place. Assemble the board first, then apply the felt. You can cut the felt around the hinges and leave a flap of felt to hide the hinges if you want.

After the felt is applied, select poster boards in complementary colors to use as mats for the papers you will mount on the display. If you will be using self-adhesive letters, consider matching that color as well. Dark-colored letters against a lighter background, or light-colored letters against a dark background are most legible.

WINNING STRATEGY #2

Plan the colors of your backboard to enhance the overall presentation. While neon and Day-Glo colors attract attention, they are hard on the eyes when there is much to be read. Likewise, using yellow on white or white on yellow is very difficult to read.

MATS AND LETTERING

You'll probably need to make two kinds of mats: one for placards (small mats bearing words like "purpose," "hypothesis," etc.) and the other for the papers you will attach to the board. Mats are important because they allow you to take papers on and off your board with minimal damage to the surface of the board (especially important with felted backboards.) To mount the mats, cut "felt savers"—scraps of cardboard slightly smaller than the mats—and staple in place where you want the mats to go. Using double-sided adhesive tape, attach the mats to the felt savers. You may use two mats of different colors, one atop the other (double matting) to enhance the display.

Figure 9.3   Single matting.

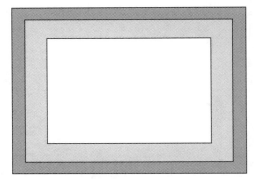

Figure 9.4   Double matting.

Try to keep the mats uniform in size, either 10-by-12 inches to accommodate papers that are 8½-by-11 inches or half that size to hold half-sheets with less information, such as the hypothesis or purpose. Papers can be attached using a glue stick or rubber cement on the back. If you have a stack of pages, such as the research paper to attach to a mat, glue the last sheet of the paper onto the mat, then run a line of glue stick across the top ½ inch of each page and glue them in order.

Figure 9.5
Assembling mats.

If you are using foam-core poster board or cardboard, instead of a wooden backboard, resist the temptation to write directly on the board. Instead, use a similar approach attaching mats and titles with double-sided tape. The appearance will be neater, more attractive, and more professional.

Don't handwrite or print titles. No matter how neat your handwriting, it is difficult to make each letter uniform, even, and straight. Instead, print the titles with a computer or use self-adhesive vinyl letters purchased at an office supply store. Be sure titles are at least 2 inches tall for easiest reading.

Figure 9.6   Make sure your type is readable from a distance.

For easy and accurate application of self-adhesive letters, stick the letters along the edge of a ruler. You can change the spacing or straighten crooked letters as much as you want while they are on the ruler. You may event want to stick them to wax paper along a straight line. Then you can carefully peel the wax paper up and stick the letters to the poster board inch by inch.

WINNING #3 STRATEGY

Be sure your titles are large enough to be read at a distance or in poor lighting.

Mount placards above each section of the backboard. You may use all or some of these: purpose, problem, hypothesis, statement of significance, abstract, background, data, graphs, statistical analysis, illustrations, photographs, charts, procedure, results, conclusion, bibliography, future studies, acknowledgments.

Figure 9.7 Mounting the mats on the backboard.

WHAT SHOULD GO WHERE?

Be strategic in arranging the elements of your project on your backboard! Your backboard is not only the billboard of your project; it is also your "cheat sheet." You will use it throughout your presentation to clarify or emphasize different points. Order the components of your project wisely on the backboard for a presentation that flows smoothly. Again, check with your teacher as a certain format may be required by the teacher or the local fair.

INSIDER'S TIP

Unless your teacher or fair require a certain format for your backboard, move from left to right in some logical fashion with your display. On the left side, place your purpose, problem, or question; hypothesis; statement of significance; and abstract. On the center panel, at the top, place data tables, graphs, illustrations, or photographs. At the bottom, your procedure and materials. On the right side, place your results, conclusion, bibliography, and plans for future studies, if any. As you present your project, you can move smoothly from one topic to the next.

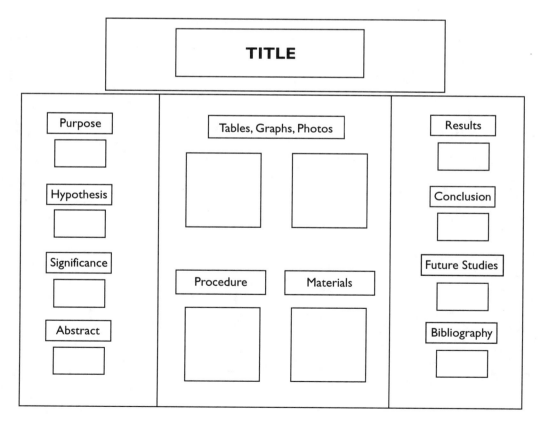

Figure 9.8 Layout of the three-panel board.

WINNING STRATEGY #4

Experiment (by now you should be good at it anyway) with the layout of your backboard until you find what is most comfortable for you. Decide what you want to display and plot out where you will put each element before you staple any placards or matting to the board.

ADDITIONAL DISPLAY ELEMENTS

If your display presentation involves a computer or video, you must still have a backboard and the rest of the display should not detract from the backboard. Videos and computer programs may supplement the backboard and the oral presentation, but should not detract from the other elements of the presentation. Models that you built are also appropriate for display. ISEF guidelines prohibit displays involving live animals, plants, microorganisms, and chemicals. Check with your teacher about any other requirements or prohibitions. A model or equipment you used in your procedure can be helpful in explaining your project, but be certain you do not leave anything unattended that could be tampered with, damaged, or stolen.

Figure 9.9 You may choose to display an original device or model you have designed and built.

Additional elements of a polished display may include a table covering, copies of the abstract to hand to judges or other viewers, the scientific paper, reprints file, and logbook. Use three-ring binders to hold the reprints file and research paper. Inside the binder, use plastic protector sheets for each page to keep them neat and clean. Reprints should be placed in some kind of binder in either alphabetical order to match the bibliography or according to subject content. Highlighting the reprints can call the judges' attention to specific points you want to make.

Some students also use additional lighting to make their display more attractive and easy to read.
Lighting can be very helpful when the fair is held in poorly lit exhibition halls or cafeterias. However, be sure your fair allows electrical connections. You will have to provide your own extension cords. The most common place to attach or incorporate lighting is through the title board.

> **WINNING STRATEGY #5**
>
> Be sure all graphs, illustrations, photographs, and drawings are labeled, titled, or self-explanatory. The board should tell the story of your project whether you are standing there or not.

Figure 9.10
Extra wings attached to hinges provide additional space and a lighted title board adds to this display.

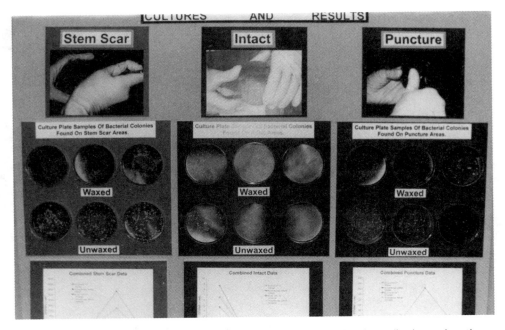

Figure 9.11   Photographs may also be used to display data that is qualitative rather than quantitative. Petri dishes are mounted over photographs.

THE FINISHED PRODUCT

Don't forget that, in the end, your backboard is simply a vehicle to display all of the work you have done. It is not the project itself, and a great backboard cannot redeem a poor project. Use your display to enhance your presentation to the judges. GULP! Presentation?! Don't worry, we're getting there. Keep reading.

WINNING STRATEGIES

1. Think of your backboard as the billboard advertising your project.
2. Plan the colors of your backboard to enhance the overall presentation. While neon and Day-Glo colors attract attention, they are hard on the eyes when there is much to be read. Likewise, using yellow on white or white on yellow is very difficult to read.
3. Be sure your titles are large enough to be read at a distance or in poor lighting.
4. Experiment (by now you should be good at it anyway) with the layout of your backboard until you find what is most comfortable for you. Decide what you want to display and plot out where you will put each element before you staple any placards or matting to the board.
5. Be sure all graphs, illustrations, photographs, and drawings are labeled, titled, or self-explanatory. The board should tell the story of your project whether you are standing there or not.

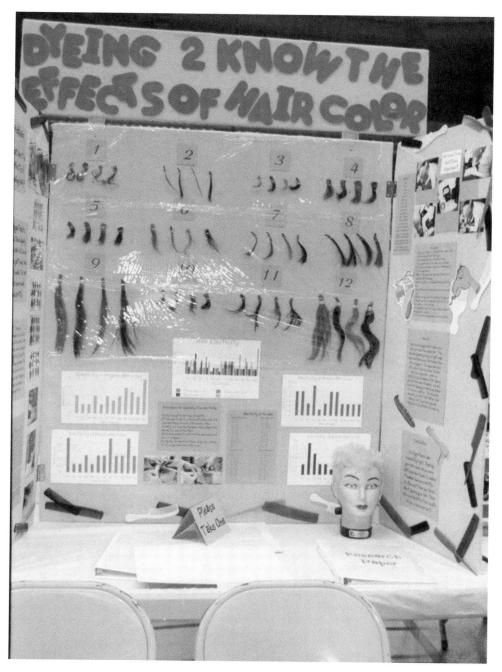

Figure 9.12   The backboard can be as individual as your project!

10

'Twas the Night Before the Fair

'Twas the night before Science fair and all through the house,

Not a creature was stirring, except the computer mouse;

Tucked away in a bedroom at a computer desk with chair,

Well past midnight, a research student labored there.

His sister was sleeping all snug in her bed,

While data, statistics, and graphs danced in his head;

The family's cat jumped up to sit on his lap,

then settled down for a long night's nap,

When on the screen before him there arose such a clatter,

The student looked up to see what was the matter.

"No, it can't be," he cried in a flash

The screen went crazy as the computer crashed.

"My graphs, my paper, my work, no, no, no!

I can't have this problem the night before the show!"

When what to his wondering eyes should appear,

But a tiny flicker of hope, a moment of cheer.

He slid the mouse and gave it a click

And the screen came back to life just as quick.

More rapid than eagles the printed pages came
And the student whistled and shouted as he exclaimed,
"Go Hewlett Packard, go Microsoft Word!
No more bugs, Scan Disk says you're cured!
From paper to spreadsheet to, now don't stall,
Print away, print away, print away ALL!"

As backboards before the fair are prepared
Set on a table with the sides squared,
And notebooks and logbooks stacked high
So, to the fair, must all the paperwork fly.
With a board full of data and conclusions, too,
The student was ready to share what he knew.

He stacked his papers neatly and bound them with a clip,
As the cat jumped down and gave him the slip.
A noise from the kitchen and he knew where Tabby went,
He rushed to the room to find a cage lid bent,
And Tabby sat next to the mouse's domicile,
Licking her lips with a satisfied smile.

"You dumb Cat!" the student cried in alarm,
"I can't believe my mouse has come to such harm.
It can't have become a midnight snack,
Give it up you bad cat, give it back!"
The student grabbed the cat's tail to give it a yank,
But the cat was quicker and the student's heart sank.

All of his work, all of his toil, gone in one swallow,
If he did win now, the victory would seem so hollow,
It had been chubby and plump, a right jolly little mouse,
The student stared forlornly at its broken house.
Without the mouse his experiments would end,
And besides, he had considered the rodent his friend.

He spoke not a word, but went on to a new chore,
He still needed to wash the pants that he wore.
And somewhere in a pile on the bed or the chair
Was a white shirt and tie he intended to wear.
Surely all could still be washed, dried, and pressed,
And he might even get a few hours rest.

The alarm went off at six that morning
And the student bolted from bed with the warning.
"I can't be late," ran through his mind
As he dashed to the laundry only to find
His shirt hanging on a hook above the sink
Clean and ready to go, but a lovely shade of pink.

Who did this horrible deed, he wanted to know
Who ruined my only shirt and gave it a rosy glow?
"The person who threw in a red shirt," mom said,
"I give up. I'm going back to bed."
"No wait, I have the answer for you.
You can borrow your dad's shirt, it's brand new."

A few minutes later, the student sprang from the car,
Glad they didn't have to drive far.
"Good luck," mom shouted as he ran to the door,
"I wonder what this folder of papers is for."

She grabbed them and hurried after her son,
Then paused at his display to admire all he had done.
"You're a winner," she said, "No matter what the place.
You've run the distance and finished the race.
That's what science research is all about.
You've learned something new, I have no doubt.
One last thing, before the judges appear,
Give it your best and come back next year!"

WINNING STRATEGIES*

1. Practice your presentation.
2. Sleep. Go to bed early.
3. Forget about the fair and don't stress out.
4. Prepare all of your equipment, whatever you need, ahead of time.
5. Reread your reprints file.
6. Decide what you're going to wear and make sure it is clean and looks nice.
7. Remember that everyone else is just as nervous as you are.
8. Go for the gold!

* Advice from research students.

11

Keeping Your Cool

The Big Day

The night before the fair you followed your teacher's advice and got a good night's sleep. The next morning, you woke up early, reviewed your notebooks one last time, and ate a good breakfast. Or, maybe you stayed up too late finishing the most up-to-date version of the abstract, tried on a half-dozen outfits, and finally settled on the shirt that had been stuffed under the bed for two weeks. You had trouble sleeping and hit the snooze button on the alarm clock three times before stumbling out of bed just as your ride pulled into the driveway. Most students fall somewhere in the middle of these two extremes!

Do not worry if on the day of the science fair you feel nervous, or even a little bit stressed. Everyone feels anxious jitters on the day of a big competition or important interview. It is natural to have a few butterflies fluttering around in your stomach. That said; there are some tried and true "stress busters" that will help you to feel confident and ready in spite of any nervousness.

THE "WHAT IF" KIT

What if you arrive the morning of the science fair and find that your backboard has fallen over and a hinge is broken? What if the light bulb behind your title board burns out? What if while waiting for your judges, you notice a glaring error on your title board?

In anticipation of these and other scenarios, assemble a "what-if kit" to take to the fair. A plastic box or shoebox works well. You may want to include items such as:

- Double-sided tape
- Liquid correction fluid
- Glue stick, rubber cement

Figure 11.1   Last minute repairs to the board.

- Scissors, stapler, ruler
- Screwdriver, pliers, hammer (if you have a wooden board)
- Extension cord, if you need electricity
- An extra light bulb if you are using lighting
- Tablecloth, if you need to provide your own
- Self-stick note paper and pen
- Extra copies of the abstract
- Adhesive bandages (for blisters from being on your feet all day)
- Extra matting, placards, and adhesive lettering (as used on your backboard)
- Anything else you might need, specific to your board/project

Ask yourself, "What if . . . ?" Anticipate minor snags (remember "Murphy's Law of Science Research!") and prepare some solutions in advance. If you know how you to respond to what *could* go wrong, you will be less likely to panic if and when something *does* go wrong.

WINNING #1 STRATEGY

Be as prepared as you can for mishaps on the day of the fair.

DRESS FOR SUCCESS

The old adage "clothing makes the person" has some merit. You will feel better about yourself and more credible if you "dress the part." Judges expect and prefer a "professional" appearance. Once again, neatness counts. You don't want to be distracted by feeling too over- or underdressed or worrying if the judge is paying more attention to your outfit than to your presentation!

Ask your science fair sponsor what is considered appropriate dress for your fair. A suit, tie, and slacks are standard apparel for young men. If last year's suit doesn't fit, nice slacks and a dress shirt, again with a tie, will be fine. For young women, a dress, suit, or skirt and blouse are appropriate. Nice slack suits may be acceptable, again consult your sponsor. Your dress should be modest; no short skirts or high thigh slits, please! Keep jewelry and exotic nails to a minimum. The project and presentation are the focus of attention today.

WINNING #2 STRATEGY

Dress neatly and professionally, and be sure to wear comfortable shoes.

Comfort is also an important aspect to consider as you plan your attire. You may be standing on your feet for several hours, so choose your shoes with care. Make certain to break in new shoes before the big day. Some science fairs are held in convention centers, others in the school gym. Temperatures vary so you may want to carry a sweater just in case the room is cold.

MEETING AND GREETING

Another way to calm your nerves is to make certain that you start off on the right foot. Treat everyone that approaches your project as a judge. In making your introduction, follow these steps for a great first impression (by the way, this works in everyday interaction as well, not just science fair competitions!)

- Take a deep breath.
- Make eye contact with the person.
- Smile.
- Greet the person appropriately, "Good morning/afternoon, etc."
- Introduce yourself, using your first name only. "My name is _____, what is yours?"
  Listen for the name.
- Respond, "It's nice to meet you, _____," while extending your hand to shake hands.

INSIDER'S TIP

Practice shaking hands with family and friends until you feel comfortable. Your grip should be firm, but not too tight. A handshake breaks the ice for you and the judge and gives you a few seconds to collect yourself before beginning your presentation.

THE MAIN SHOW

Once you've introduced yourself, you can launch right into your presentation. State the title of your project. Then, after a brief pause, grab the judge's attention by stating the significance of your project before rattling off anything else. You want to demonstrate right away why your research is important (the "who cares?" part of your project).

WINNING STRATEGY #3

Be enthusiastic about your project. Your excitement about your project will be contagious. One judge commented that she considers the student's enthusiasm as important as the presentation.

ONE STUDENT'S PRESENTATION

Mary has just finished introducing herself. She begins her presentation, "In the course of my research I studied 'The Prognostic Significance of DNA Ploidy in Prostatic Cancer.' In the United States alone, sixty thousand men will be diagnosed with prostate cancer this year and 10 percent of them will die from that disease. I wanted to show that the DNA ploidy of prostatic cancer makes a difference in the staging of the disease. Studying the DNA ploidy would enable doctors to know which cancers require more aggressive treatment."

In these few sentences, Mary has described her title and hypothesis. More importantly, she has shown her judge why this research is significant and made the judge eager to learn more. She has probably incited several questions in the judge's mind, such as "What is DNA ploidy?" And, "How do doctors currently stage prostate cancer?" "How is this disease treated?"

Mary must not disappoint her judge. She will answer these questions naturally as she next discusses what DNA ploidy is (background) and how she studied it (her procedure).

You can anticipate the questions a judge will ask by practicing your presentation with your parents or teacher. Ask them to tell you what kinds of questions they would ask you if they were judges. You can insert that information into your presentation before you even get to the fair. Follow the statement of significance with a brief discussion of the background information, your hypothesis, and procedure. Generalize the procedure. It isn't necessary to mention every step. The judge will stop you with a question if something isn't clear.

You can pause periodically and ask if the judge has any questions, but you may also march through your presentation without pausing if that is more comfortable for you. Either way works well for the judges. The judge will interrupt if there is a question or the need for clarification. After describing the procedure, tell the judge what you found (the results) but you do not need to go into a detailed statistical analysis of the results. The judge will look at the statistics and graphs and ask questions if he doesn't understand them. Finally, state your conclusions. Explain whether your hypothesis was supported or not, accepted or rejected, and describe any plans for future studies. If you have copies of the abstract, this is a good time to offer one. Judges will probably already have one, but you may have updated it.

When you have finished your presentation, invite questions.

> **WINNING STRATEGY #4**
>
> Practice your presentation ahead of time so that you are not reading everything straight off of your backboard. Use the backboard for clarification if the judge has a question and refer back to it for visual representation of your results (through graphs, photos, etc.).

INSIDER'S TIP

The judge may ask you a question to which you simply don't know the answer. Don't panic and whatever you do, don't fake an answer. The best response is (you guessed it) to be honest. Respond simply: "I don't know, but I will get the answer. Can you visit me later?" Write the question down and be certain to follow through and do your best to find the answer.

You can also enlist the judge's support of your work. Judges want your project to be a success and a good learning experience for you. Ask how you might improve your project or presentation. And learn from each judge. One judge pointed out that there is an advantage to being the last judge of the day. By that time, the savvy student has perfected the presentation and anticipated the questions.

The judges return from year to year, and chances are you'll have the same one again if you continue in science research. Next year, point out to the judge how much the advice for improvement helped you.

Don't ramble or try to fill silences. The judge has an assignment to be certain all of your components are present. She will want to see your logbook, reprints file, and paper. Make them available, but let the judge flip through them. Show the judge all the reasons you have an award-winning project. When the judge is finished, thank her.

There may be long periods of time before another judge or visitor comes along. If seating is available, feel free to sit, but remain alert, ready to jump right back up and into your presentation.

INSIDER'S TIP

Definite Don'ts during the Fair:

- Don't chew gum. If it is permitted, you may have a glass of water and sip it as needed.

- Don't give excuses. If your plants died because of an unexpected power outage, tell the judge that. But, don't tell the judge your three-year-old brother poured fruit juice on your log, or that you couldn't do what you originally planned to do because your teacher wouldn't let you build a nuclear device at school and so you had to do this dumb project he/she suggested.

- Don't read books, study, do homework, gossip with your neighbor, write love letters, talk on a cellular phone, or play games between judges. It may be boring, but stay with the project and be attentive. If you have to leave for a few moments, ask your teacher for permission.

THE UGLY JUDGE

Every fair has one. The judge who is an expert and wants everyone to know it. The judge who doesn't ask questions, or who asks too many questions about every minute and obscure detail. The judge who argues with your results. The judge who criticizes and belittles. The judge who isn't fair. The judge who spends five minutes with you and a half-hour at the next project.

Enough said. At some point in your research career, you will probably meet this judge. We wish it weren't true, but sometimes this happens. What should you do? Treat him as you have every other judge. Be friendly, enthusiastic, and confident with your presentation. *Never argue with a judge.* Even if the judge is wrong. Even if your research shows something completely different. Even if you know more about the subject. Assume his intentions are good. He is volunteering his time to be there. And, the next judge will be better.

WINNING STRATEGY #5

Never argue with a judge, even if he is wrong.

RELAX!

Above all else, enjoy this day! It is a day for which you have worked very hard. Maintain your sense of humor and perspective and minor emergencies, broken hinges, and ugly judges won't cause you to lose your cool. Remember: your science fair project's success is based on so much more than this one day. Keep taking deep breaths and keep smiling at each new judge or passerby that stops to discuss your research. Don't allow nervousness to prevent you from enjoying and learning from this challenging experience!

WINNING STRATEGY #6

Relax, keep a sense of humor, and try to enjoy yourself!

WINNING STRATEGIES

1. Be as prepared as you can for mishaps on the day of the fair.
2. Dress neatly and professionally, and be sure to wear comfortable shoes.
3. Be enthusiastic about your project. Your excitement about your project will be contagious. One judge commented that she considers the student's enthusiasm as important as the presentation.
4. Practice your presentation ahead of time so that you are not reading everything straight off of your backboard. Use the backboard for clarification if the judge has a question and refer back to it for visual representation of your results (through graphs, photos, etc.).
5. Never argue with a judge, even if he is wrong.
6. Relax, keep a sense of humor, and try to enjoy yourself!

12

"Your Honor . . ."

Who Are the Judges and What Do They Want?

You can practice presenting your research to friends and family members, but you already know those people, and a science fair judge will be a stranger to you. You can answer your parents' questions, but the judge could ask any question under the sun. You know what your teacher is looking for, but how can you know what a judge wants to see and know about your project?

These concerns are common. However, just as you might prepare for an interview or a presentation, you can prepare for judging by considering who the judges are, what they are looking for, and how you can learn from your interaction with them.

Figure 12.1 Judge checking display.

WHO ARE THE JUDGES?

While you may not have ever met the person approaching you with their clipboard and "Judge" nametag, there are a few facts you should know about them. Science fair judges volunteer their time to participate in the fair because they care about students and science research. Even at the top levels of science fair competition, judges are not paid or otherwise recognized for this service. They are simply there because they are interested in your project.

> **WINNING #1 STRATEGY**
> Make a friend of anyone who shows interest in your project. That casual visitor may be a special awards judge or a scientist who might be your mentor next year.

Aside from their genuine desire to work with students, science fair judges may have little in common. They represent a cross section of the local scientific, educational, and industrial communities. They are teachers, professors, engineers, computer programmers, physicians, nurses, scientists, pathologists, lab technicians, psychologists, dentists, veterinarians, physicists, mathematicians, horticulturists, experts in every one of the up to fourteen categories of projects. The judges may be alumni of your school and it may help you to realize that once upon a time, they were kids doing their own science fair projects.

At the Intel International Science and Engineering Fair, all of the judges have a Ph.D. or equivalent degree and at least eight years relevant experience. At all levels of competition, the judges volunteer their time, and pay whatever travel or personal expenses they incur. A board of ten scientists from different disciplines judges the Science Talent Search candidates.

The judges are also mentors who work daily with student researchers. They are anxious to encourage you, teach you, help you, sponsor you, and invite you to look at the world in a whole new way.

INSIDER'S TIP

Spend a minute asking the judge about his background as it relates to your project. It may help to know if the last time he heard anything about your topic was thirty years ago in college or if he works in this field every day.

WHAT DO JUDGES WANT?

> **WINNING #2 STRATEGY**
> Get to know something about the judge's background.

Now that you know a bit about who the judges are, what exactly do they expect from you? Junior and senior high research students were asked, "What do you think science fair judges are looking for?" One student answered, "I don't know. I'm clueless!" Don't be discouraged if you feel the same way.

What are judges looking for? Do standards differ from category to category, or are there common criteria that judges use to evaluate projects, regardless of the area of research?

The judges have a checklist of the required components for a project. If the necessary pieces (scientific paper, data treatment, logbook, reprints file, and backboard) are missing, the student cannot progress to the next level of competition. In addition to this, the science fair may have a standardized scoring or rating form that judges use to evaluate projects regardless of category. These forms may vary from fair to fair; however the basic components that judges look for in science fair projects are universal, including:

- how well the student followed the scientific method
- the detail and accuracy of research documented in the data
- whether experimental procedures were used in the best possible ways

Some of the subjective criteria judges consider include:

- creativity
- scientific thought
- subject knowledge
- thoroughness
- skill
- clarity

The objective criteria judges look at include:

- data treatment
- use of statistical analysis
- the scientific paper
- the display, backboard, reprints file, and logbook

This list may seem daunting, however remember that the judges aren't looking for perfection as much as they are potential. One judge said, "More than anything, I look for passion for the project."

The judges are instructed in advance about how to evaluate projects. Ways in which the judges apply their instructions will vary from person to person. Some judges look mainly for the significance of the project. How does it apply to real-life situations? Others are interested in your thoroughness. Did you research all aspects of the project? Do your results correspond well to the hypothesis? In other words, did you follow through on what you intended to do? The judge may ask you questions such as, "What didn't you do?" "What would be your next step?"

The judges are also looking for originality in your project. Did you do the work yourself? How much help did you receive from a mentor, sponsoring scientist, teacher, or parent? It will be very obvious to the judges if you have not done the work yourself. Of course, you may need to learn new techniques and have someone demonstrate them to you. However, the learning part should not be your entire experimentation. You should be able to show that you've performed the procedure independently.

You will be judged on how you used the technology available to you. Did you use the spell-check function of the computer? Did you use the Internet as well as a library for research? Are you aware of other researchers' work on your topic? Do you have a variety of sources for your background research?

Judges appreciate students who can talk freely and clearly about their project. Don't worry about a memorized presentation. As one judge said, "I don't mind if a student has to pause, I'll wait. I don't want rote memory or for them to just read off a chart on their board."

Explain your project as if you were sharing it with a friend. Knowledge and enthusiasm go a long way toward impressing the judges. Judges want to know that a student has learned something from participating.

> **WINNING STRATEGY #3**
>
> Find out as much as you can about what the judges expect from your project.

INSIDER'S TIP

If possible, obtain a copy of the judging form from your fair director ahead of time. Rate yourself. What are some of the areas in which you could improve? What are your strengths?

WHAT CAN YOU LEARN FROM YOUR JUDGES?

Each time you are interviewed by a judge you have an opportunity to learn something new about yourself and your project. Keep a small notebook or legal pad handy so that you can jot down notes. Judges often make helpful suggestions for improvement of your presentation or project. They might suggest books or articles that you could read, or local experts in your field that you might contact. Listen attentively and write these ideas down—in the nervousness and excitement of the moment, these tips can be easily forgotten.

> **WINNING STRATEGY #4**
>
> Listen to any suggestions the judges may have for your project and write down these ideas. If you advance to the next level of competition, be sure to make these changes in your project or presentation.

After you meet with each judge, evaluate the interview. Write down the aspects of your presentation that you thought were very effective or what you felt good about. Jot reminders for improvement, like "Remember to make eye contact next time," or "I need to explain my statistical analysis more clearly." As you review these notes you will find that your presentation improves from interview to interview.

MEETING FACE-TO-FACE

No matter how much you prepare for judging, having butterflies in your stomach is natural and unavoidable. Nearly every student experiences nervousness when faced with presenting his or her research to a judge. Take a deep breath, smile, and take the judge's hand in a firm handshake. You might even find it helpful to admit it; "I'm sorry, but I'm very nervous." The first judge of the day is always the most difficult, and judges know and understand that as well. Don't worry if you stumble or falter at times. Remember that while a calm, logical, clear, and concise presentation may assist the judges in their decision-making, it is the quality of your work and how you applied the scientific method that matter most.

Your project does not exist in a vacuum. It is one of several or many in your category and in the fair. First, it will be judged on its own merits, then compared to others in the category, then possibly, to other first-place projects in all categories for a "Best of Show" award.

INSIDER'S TIP

Typical Questions a Judge Will Ask:

- How or why did you get interested in this topic?
- Do you intend to continue working in this area or pursue future education in science?
- What practical applications does your work have?
- What would you change about your experimentation if you could do it all over again?
- What did you learn from this project?

WINNING STRATEGIES

1. Make a friend of anyone who shows interest in your project. That casual visitor may be a special awards judge or a scientist who might be your mentor next year.
2. Get to know something about the judge's background.
3. Find out as much as you can about what the judges expect from your project.
4. Listen to any suggestions the judges may have for your project and write down these ideas. If you advance to the next level of competition, be sure to make these changes in your project or presentation.

13

Is There Life After the Science Fair?

After the Big Day

It is the day after the awards ceremony. Perhaps you are still in shock over your "Best of Show" ribbon. You may now know that you'll be advancing to further competition. Your mind is racing with plans to run more experimental trials, improve your backboard, follow up with that judge who gave you his card. "I can't believe I won," you are saying. "I can't wait until next year's fair!"

Or you might have earned a lower place than you'd hoped. All of your friends took second and first place ribbons while you earned a fourth prize. You're feeling angry and bitter and you never want to see your backboard or logbook again in your life. You feel like the whole year's work was a waste. "I'm never doing that again," you tell yourself.

Whatever you're feeling, don't make any decisions yet about next year's fair. The days following the science fair bring mixed emotions for most students, regardless of whether they took first or last prize. You have been working on your project for months, and in some cases, years. The few weeks before the fair were frantic and exciting and you spent a great deal of time preparing for this one event. It is natural to feel relief and disappointment when it is all over. Try to avoid making a rash decision during this time, such as "I'm never doing that again," or, "Sign me up for the next three years!" Give yourself a few weeks to allow the dust to settle. You may find that you feel very differently about science research and the fair experience two weeks later.

DEFINING PERSONAL SUCCESS

You know that it is important to win and lose gracefully. Chances are, you are more likely to have to do the latter. In science fairs, as in most competitions in life, a limited percentage of the competitors win first prize, or any prize at all. While winning first place is a wonderful goal to set for yourself, it is not always the way to define a successful science fair project.

One student recalls a very disappointing fair experience. "It was my tenth grade year and I'd worked so hard on my project. I thought for certain I was going to win a first or second place in my category. Then, I had a very ugly judge. He was so mean! I lost my temper with him. I won a third place that year. At first I was angry and bitter, but it also made me all the more determined to come back the next year. That year I took a second place. I had to decide that winning first place wasn't going to mean success to me. Learning and persevering were. Finally, the following year I won first place, Best of Show, and an ISEF bid. It was so incredible. But I don't think I would have appreciated that win if I hadn't been losing all those years before."

This student made a very important decision: winning first place wasn't going to define success for her. She set a *goal* of first prize, but her definition of *success* was something very different.

What should you consider in your personal definition of success? It may include aspects such as:

- Learning something new.
- Improving public speaking skills.
- Persevering over difficulties, like plants that won't grow from seed or handling the ugly judge.
- Acquiring computer skills.
- Understanding statistical analysis.
- Using the scientific method.
- Making a connection with the scientific community.
- Adding this experience to your resume for college applications.

Write down your own personal definition of success in science research before the science fair. Writing your own definition will allow you to win gracefully because you'll know that you have won something far greater than a ribbon. It will allow you to lose gracefully because you'll know that you're still a winner in what you have gained from the experience.

YOUR SCIENCE FAIR PROJECT: THE SEQUEL

Perhaps you've given yourself time to consider everything that you've learned and have discovered an experimental subject about which you are passionate. Or, your experimentation left you with a million questions that you want to investigate further. Your project may be a good candidate for a second-year study.

If you are considering pursuing your topic into a second or even third year of research, there are a few aspects of continuing research that you should keep in mind:

- A continuing study cannot be a repetition of the original project. Judges may even be more critical of continuing studies and will definitely ask you, "How is this year's experimentation markedly different from what you investigated last year?"

- A second- or third-year study should still involve every step of the scientific method. You'll need to do background research on the new aspects of your experimentation, develop a new hypothesis, experimental procedure, etc.

- Save materials from the prior study—abstract, research paper, reprints file, etc.—and have them on hand for the science fair in case a judge has a question about the past year's experimentation.

Remember, a project that is not scientifically sound or that is boring to you will not be any better in a second or third year. You may also learn from the experiment that your question mutates and changes over time into something related, but quite different.

One student was interested in phytoplankton and whether their absorption of carbon dioxide influences the "greenhouse effect" and global warming. In her first-year research, she learned about ozone layer depletion related to the "greenhouse effect" and increases in ultraviolet radiation. The following year, she studied the effects of different ultraviolet radiation levels on phytoplankton populations. The third year, after learning about the effects of ultraviolet radiation on humans, she studied skin cancer.

Was this a continuing study? No. Each year's project, however, opened a door to a new, but related project. Each year stood independently and didn't build on the previous year's research and experimentation.

INSIDER'S TIP

A multiyear project may ask the same question but cannot repeat the same hypothesis or experimentation. You should not simply do more runs of the same project from year to year.

PUBLISHING AND PATENTS

Consider publishing your work or filing a patent application if you have invented something new or a new use for existing technology. Your mentor may be able to assist you to find the best publisher for your paper and to prepare it for publication.

AFTER THE LAST FAIR

You stripped and stored your board for the last time, tossed your logbook into the closet, and put your notebooks on the shelf. Award ribbons and plaques are hung on the bulletin board and bedroom wall and science research is a memory eclipsed by the excitement of graduation.

What's next?

For the next few years you may stop when you hear a news report and think, "That would make a great science fair project." You might recall your own projects and wish you had pursued different angles. You might take your studies further into college. Shawn Nobles studied tree rings in fourth grade and went on to receive her bachelor's and master's degrees in environmental studies and, now as a naturalist, leads a program for inner city youth teaching them about animals and trees and nature. Jeremy Reis, whose eighth grade project dealt with artificial intelligence, took his interest in computers through college and into a career in the business world. Tyler White uses some of his years of experience with botany projects as he works in his own nursery. Science research can point you toward your future studies and career.

Your experiences can lead to other opportunities as well. One of the authors of this book used her research project to apply for the Education First Ambassador Program and received a ten-day trip to Europe. Other students have found that the discipline and skills they learned in science research have helped them in other activities, such as Odyssey of the Mind, Future Problem-Solvers competitions, Math Olympiad, and so on. Participation in science research is also an important advantage when applying for college admission and scholarships.

RETURNING AS A JUDGE

There is nothing more rewarding than coming back to science research as a judge. Start with the elementary classes. Contact the administrator of the school and offer to help as a judge at their next science fair. Your call will be routed to the appropriate person and your offer received with gratitude. When it comes time to be a judge, remember everything you learned from being a student. Be patient and gentle with these young researchers. Your encouragement will make all the difference in their continuing interest in science research. Avoid being too critical—their projects won't be the same caliber as the level in which you last competed. The most important aspect is their enthusiasm toward science. Be fair in your judging and quick with your praise.

You may also want to judge at the junior-senior high level and you probably know the person to contact for that fair. If you were the kind of student the fair director enjoyed having in the fair every year, you will be welcomed to return as a judge. Look and act the part. Students will consider you a mentor. Wear a suit or neat and clean outfit. Write notes on presentations and projects. You may visit twenty or thirty and will have to remember the details of each one in order to rank them.

Again, use your own experience wisely by being the kind of judge you wish you had. Give helpful criticism sandwiched between favorable comments. Avoid the tendency to share your own experiences, procedure, or project results. Instead, ask questions and gently guide the students toward new discoveries. Always comment on the student's potential. Most students have the potential to do great things when inspired and you may be the person to encourage them.

WINNING STRATEGY

Don't make winning first place the only measure of your success. Think of what you will get from science research and the fair whether you win or lose.

14

A Letter to Parents

Whether your student has chosen to participate in science research or it was a mandatory assignment, your attitude and assistance can make or break your son or daughter's experience. First, how should you react? Be proud. This is a difficult, but very rewarding undertaking for your child. No other academic competition requires so much intense effort over many months. No other extracurricular activity involves so many diverse skills. If you have looked at the rest of this book, you will know that your child must develop research skills, write a paper, perform an experiment, and develop a visual and oral presentation. He will need your support and help.

Therein often lie the problems. Unfortunately, junior and senior high students are at the age where they don't want parents' help or involvement. You'll need open lines of communication, wisdom, and patience to know when you should step in to help.

GET INVOLVED EARLY

When your daughter first comes home and announces, "I'm doing a science fair project," discuss then what her expectations are of your role. You might start with an expression of how pleased you are ("Sounds like fun."). Do not relate the story of your eighth grade project.

Next, ask your child if she has any idea what topic she might like to research. Listen. Don't suggest. You can point your child in certain directions without suggesting a specific topic. For example, you might say, "You've always liked computers, is there something in that area you could do?" or, "Is there something from your science classes you'd like to investigate more?"

This is an excellent opportunity to allow your child to further develop her natural talents. Be creative—your child is not limited to hard sciences (what you typically recall when you think of a science fair project). If your daughter really enjoys music, she could study how listening to classical tunes affects prematurely born babies. If your son is interested in video games he might develop a research project using his favorite video games.

Remember that your child's interests are most likely different from your own. The easiest suggestions for projects you can think of probably relate to your field or profession. However, these may not be best suited to your child's interests or talents.

If your child is clueless (which is most likely), ask (don't suggest) if there is someone he can think of in the community who might be a mentor. It is amazing how kids who don't want their parents' ideas will accept them from anyone else. All you have to do is open your address or phone book and check your local resources.

- For a botany project, try a local nursery.

- Chemistry projects don't always involve the lab. Construction contractors know a lot about cement, its application in specific building projects, and the conditions under which it fails.

- Biochemistry applications are also prevalent in many communities. Pest-control and lawn services use chemicals that may prompt a student's study.

- The local water company may have employees who test and maintain the water's purity and safety.

- If there is a park, there may be a naturalist on staff who can suggest an environmental project.

- Physicians, pharmacists, dentists, veterinarians, and hospital lab technicians may provide direction for projects in medicine, zoology, biology, biochemistry or microbiology.

- A local college biology or chemistry department or research laboratory might suggest topics and provide mentors.

ASSIST WITH TIME MANAGEMENT

Once a topic for the project is chosen, help your child develop a timeline. Determine when crucial elements of the project are due. Mark important dates on a calendar, but refrain from nagging about deadlines. One or two reminders as the date approaches will have to do.

Ultimately, your child is responsible and failure to complete the project is no reflection on your parenting. (Unfortunately, neither is success in the project. You can brag when your child wins, but no one will give you a ribbon for being the winner's mom or dad.)

Discuss with your child how you can help him during the research and experimentation phases of his project. For example, one year, my daughter worked with a scientist 100 miles from our home. She wasn't yet old enough to drive, so we had to work around the scientist's lab schedule, her school schedule, and my work schedule. Several Friday afternoon and Saturday morning trips accomplished the experimentation. If your student is dependent on you for transportation, you need to know up front what time commitment will be needed.

What other skills and help might be required of you? Over the years, I have photographed anti-bubbles in a homemade aquarium in the kitchen, visited lakes to gather duck feathers, and even plucked feathers from a dead and frozen duck at a vet's office. I have taken a test to determine whether I am left- or right-brain dominant, sat through an organic chemistry lecture, and chaperoned seventh graders at a science exhibit. I have applied felt, stapled, glued, taped, cleaned, and carried numerous backboards.

There may also be expenses involved in research and this should be discussed early in the project. Does the school require the student to provide a backboard? Where will experimentation be performed? What supplies will your child need to purchase? Where and how will she write her paper? Does she need a home computer, calculator, or special software?

ASSIST WITH RESEARCH AND EXPERIMENTATION

Be prepared to drive your child to the library and make sure she has access to the Internet either there or at home. She may also need your assistance thinking of the terms to use while searching. Ask her questions. If you happen to come across a related article or source in your readings, share it with her. Supervise her experimentation if necessary. Even if you know nothing about the procedure, you can follow what she is doing.

BE A PROOFREADER AND AUDIENCE

Offer to read her paper and abstract, but don't be offended if she declines. Sometimes, parents are the worst critics. Remember, you are reading only to catch spelling and grammatical errors, not to rephrase her words.

Listen to her presentation. Ask the kinds of questions a judge might ask. Help her organize her thoughts. The more times she has to explain her project, the better she'll do when it comes time for the fair.

BE YOUR CHILD'S CHEERLEADER

Every kid needs a cheerleader parent, not a caretaker parent. Be supportive, but stay on the sidelines. Science fair is the student's competition, not yours. Don't embarrass your child. Don't compare other students' projects to your childs in a critical way. "Just look at John's board. Why didn't you use a computer in your display?" Tell the student you are very proud of his work and, in your eyes, he's number one.

Don't criticize a judge, a result, or a decision. Yes, from your perspective, your child's project is, by far, the best and any result other than first place is a gross injustice. But, keep that opinion to yourself. The judges may have seen something in their interviews that you don't know. Even if their decision is wrong, your job as a parent is to teach your child how to accept losing as gracefully as winning. Commiserate without blaming.

YOU CAN'T RELIVE YOUR YOUTH

Above all else, remember that this is your student's project and not yours. Don't base everything on your own ninth grade science project. Life was different when you were a student. I am reminded of that every time I look at the chemistry lab's table of periodic elements. There were fewer of them when I took high school chemistry. You may have done a project that won first place at the International Science and Engineering Fair; you may have written a best-selling book about it and a movie may have been made about it. But, your kid doesn't care. This is *his* project, his challenge, and his life. Someday, perhaps, he will even thank you (but, don't expect it!).

WINNING STRATEGIES

Your attitude toward your child's project will greatly influence his/her science research experience. Approach this event with patience, flexibility, and a sense of humor. Expect success from your student (and remember that this doesn't always equal a first place ribbon).

Appendix A
Researching Online

The Internet can be a tremendous help to the science research student, but only when she understands what it is, what it isn't, and how to use it. It is a network that links one computer to another, and another, and another—next door or in the next city. In seconds, you can communicate with someone on the other side of the world. The Internet itself does not contain or carry information.

There is a great deal of information available through the Internet, but it is not a giant library or encyclopedia. Everything was posted by someone for some reason. The articles and information may be someone's life work and research or it may be their theories, wishes, or dreams. There are no editors or publishers to verify facts nor are there required standards. If you do choose to use it for serious research, you need to realize that what you find may not be complete or entirely accurate. Using a wide variety of resources is always the most balanced way to conduct background research.

When you go to the library, your first stop might be the card catalogue (or the computerized version of it). You need to have an idea what you are looking for before you open the drawer or turn on the computer. Think of the Internet as a card catalogue. The Internet walks you from the "card catalogue" to the "bookshelf." In both the library and on the Internet, you must still "open the book," study it, evaluate the information, and decide what you can use.

Begin with a simple search. The broad categories of projects, such as "botany," "health," "environment" will return too many sites. Select a few keywords related to your project. For example, for the gerbil and maze project, use "gerbil." For a project involving a plant, don't use "plant," but rather the name of the specific plant. Then, think of several synonyms if possible. And, be sure your spelling is correct. Always type the search word in lower case. Capital letters return fewer sites as some search engines don't accept capital letters.

Next try a phrase search. List several terms in the proper order and enclosed in quotations. The sites returned will have that phrase in that order. For example, "gerbil food" or "fertilizer for tomato plants."

A more complicated search is a Boolean search in which you tie terms together with a + (plus) sign. Do not put any spaces between the word and the + sign. The article or site must contain all of those words. For example, "gerbil+food+maze," or "onion+fertilizer." If you do not get any sources, you may have narrowed the search too much and need to be more general.

For a broader search, try using truncation. Search with the first few letters of the word. For example, type in "librar" and you will get sites with library, librarian, or libraries.

So, how do you go about searching the World Wide Web for the information you want? There are hundreds of search vehicles available to you and a basic understanding of how they differ will help you choose the right one.

MOST COMMONLY USED SEARCH VEHICLES

Yahoo!   www.yahoo.com

Alta Vista   www.altavista.com

InfoSeek   www.infoseek.com

Excite   www.excite.com

Lycos   www.lycos.com

HotBot   www.hotbot.com

WebCrawler   www.webcrawler.com

Northern Light   www.northernlight.com

Google   www.google.com

Alta Vista search engine is one of the largest, most powerful, and easy to use World Wide Web engines. You may type one or two keywords, use the Boolean method, or truncated terms. Infoseek is ranked as one of the top search engines and also allows you to use Boolean search, and truncated terms. Excite is especially easy for beginners because it accepts phrases that are not specific. On the other hand, Lycos requires more specific keywords be used and does not allow Boolean searches. WebCrawler was one of the first search engines and is still easy to use.

You may want to visit several of the search engines to find all of the resources that are available online. You will waste a great deal of time unless you choose your keywords carefully and keep the search as narrow as possible.

ASK JEEVES

One way to narrow the search is to use the Ask Jeeves search engine at www.askjeeves.com, which allows you to ask a question and immediately returns all the possible resources, including other search engines. Askjeeves may also find a specialty search engine for you when you ask, "Where can I find a search engine for _____?" (Fill in the blank with the topic of your project.)

Just as at the library, the Internet also contains some magazines, newspapers, and periodicals. Frequently, you have to subscribe and may have to pay for these. Try these two sites:

The Internet Public Library at ipl.sils.umich.edu/

Online periodicals at the Electronic Newsstand at www.enews.com

Because the information is all right there on your computer, it is tempting to cut and paste information straight into your paper. This is plagiarism. Print the information on paper, read and paraphrase it as you would with a book. (See Chapter 8 for our discussion on plagiarism and how to avoid it.) Remember to cite Internet sources as you would other sources.

Feel free to use the Internet in your research as long as you remember to keep the search narrow so you don't waste time, verify the information with other sources, and credit sources appropriately, including the date and time of access.

WINNING STRATEGY

Try to keep the search as narrow as possible, and learn to filter out sites that are not relevant to your research.

Appendix B
References for Studying Statistics

Gonick, Larry and Woollcott Smith. *The Cartoon Guide to Statistics*. New York: HarperCollins, 1994.

Koosis, Donald. Statistics. *A Self-Teaching Guide*. New York: John Wiley & Sons, 1997.

Krieger, Melanie Jacobs. *Using Statistics in Science Projects*. New York: F. Watts, 1991.

Mitchell, Robert P. *Measurement and Data Analysis*. New York: New Readers Press, 1996.

Slavin, Steven. *Chances Are: The Only Statistics Book You'll Ever Need*. Maryland: Madison Books, 1998.

Wagner, Susan. *Introduction to Statistics*. New York: HarperPerennial, 1992.

Glossary

Abstract—A one-page summary of your science fair project; limited in length by ISEF guidelines to a maximum of 250 words.

Array—An arrangement of data in a table.

Backboard—The display (generally consisting of three panels) of your science fair project.

Background—General researched information concerning your topic of study or experimental question.

Bibliography—A list of source materials or references compiled during research of your topic, generally appearing at the end of the research paper.

Citation, Textual—A reference within the body of your research paper to a specific source, book, author, etc.

Confidence Intervals—The known relationship between the percentage of data that fall within certain standard deviations from the mean.

Control—The experimental group that is not changed in order to serve as a standard of comparison in experimentation.

Data—The information (often in the form of numbers or statistics) derived through experimentation.

Footnotes—A reference or citation appearing at the bottom of a page of your research paper.

Graph—A diagram or visual representation of your data.

Hypothesis—Your prediction of the results of your experiment.

Inoculation Techniques—Procedures used to grow microorganisms on agar plates.

ISEF—The International Science and Engineering Fair held annually.

Logbook—A detailed, chronological record of research and experimentation kept by researchers.

Mean—The number that represents the mathematical average of a data set.

Median—The number that represents the midpoint of a data set.

Mode—The number that appears most frequently in a data set.

Null Hypothesis—A negative expression or the opposite of your prediction of the results of your experiment.

Petri Plate—A shallow circular dish with a loose-fitting lid, used to grow microorganisms.

Plagiarism—The representation of someone else's work as your own.

Practical Application—A statement of the valuable implications of your experimentation.

Procedure—A step-by-step plan or recipe describing how to perform the experiment.

Protocol—The rules for experimentation issued by ISEF.

Run—An experimental trial.

Scientific Method—The set of problem-solving steps used by scientists.

Scientific Review Committee—A state-level review board that sets standards for projects and must approve them when certain chemicals, biological specimens or procedures are used.

Standard Deviation—A measure of the spread of the data from the mean.

Statistical Analysis—The gathering, display, summary, and comparison of raw data (such as a list of numbers) to gain meaningful information and to communicate your experimental results to others.

Sterilize—To destroy living germs or microorganisms on an object or surface.

Title Board—The part of your backboard bearing the title or experimental question.

Typical Values—Reference in statistics to one value that represents all of the data values, namely the mean, median, or mode.

Variable—The experimental group that is changed and compared to the control.

Index

38004000604197

Henderson, Joyce.

507
Hen

Strategies for
winning science fair
projects

$10.96

DATE DUE	BORROWER'S NAME	ROOM NO.
JA 3 1 '07	Georgie Alexis	212

38004000604197
Henderson, Joyce.

507
Hen

Strategies for
winning science fair
projects